God's Daily Promises
for Men

DAILY WISDOM FROM GOD'S WORD

BOOKS IN THE
GOD'S DAILY PROMISES SERIES

God's Daily

PROMISES

for Men

DAILY WISDOM
FROM GOD'S WORD

Tyndale House Publishers, Inc.

Carol Stream, Illinois

Visit Tyndale's exciting Web site at www.tyndale.com.

TYNDALE and Tyndale's quill logo are registered trademarks of Tyndale House Publishers, Inc.

New Living Translation, NLT, and the New Living Translation logo are registered trademarks of Tyndale House Publishers, Inc.

God's Daily Promises for Men: Daily Wisdom from God's Word

Copyright © 2007 by Ron Beers. All rights reserved.

Cover artwork copyright © by iStockphoto.com. All rights reserved.

General Editors: Ron Beers and Amy Mason

Contributing Editor: Rebecca Beers

Contributing Writers: V. Gilbert Beers, Ronald A. Beers, Brian R. Coffey, Jonathan Farrar, Jonathan Gray, Sean A. Harrison, Sandy Hull, Rhonda K. O'Brien, and Douglas J. Rumford

Designed by Julie Chen

Edited by Michal Needham

Scripture quotations are taken from the *Holy Bible,* New Living Translation, copyright © 1996, 2004. Used by permission of Tyndale House Publishers, Inc., Carol Stream, Illinois 60188. All rights reserved.

ISBN 978-1-4143-1232-3

Printed in the United States of America

15 14 13 12 11 10
 8   7   6   5   4   3

INTRODUCTION

Why did God make so many promises? Maybe it's
because he wants to show you how much you can
really trust him. Maybe he is so interested in you that
he is trying to get your attention with each amazing promise he makes, wanting to show you just how
much you have to look forward to as you travel
through life. This unique book presents more
than 365 of these incredible promises, at least
one for every day of the year. All these promises
will come true—or have already come true. You
simply have to decide whether you want to be
part of them or not.

Imagine that every morning you could be
inspired by a promise from God's Word and then
live the rest of the day with either the expectation that God will fulfill that promise or the
confidence that comes from a promise
already fulfilled. *God's Daily Promises for Men*
is designed to inspire you in just that way.

Every page is dated, making the book easy
to use. First, read the promise from God.
Think about it. Let it soak in. Then read
the short devotional note to help you look
at your day differently because of God's
promise. Finally, read the question at the
end to encourage and motivate you to
trust that this promise was meant for you.
Claim the promise as your own with the confidence

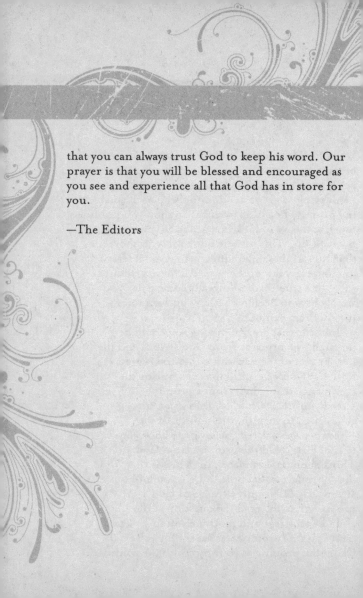

that you can always trust God to keep his word. Our prayer is that you will be blessed and encouraged as you see and experience all that God has in store for you.

—The Editors

January

BEGINNINGS

TODAY'S PROMISE

This means that anyone who belongs to Christ has become a new person. The old life is gone; a new life has begun!
—2 CORINTHIANS 5:17

TODAY'S THOUGHT

New beginnings give you fresh vision and purpose, renew your energy, and stimulate you to greater passion in areas where you have slipped into complacency. The most important new beginning in your life is when you change directions and start to follow Jesus. When you believe in Jesus Christ, you are not simply turning over a new leaf—you are literally re-created. You are transformed on the inside, which changes the way you act on the outside. You begin a new life!

TODAY'S PLAN

Have you allowed Jesus to make you a new person? How will that transform your thoughts and actions this year?

VISION

TODAY'S PROMISE

"My thoughts are nothing like your thoughts," says the LORD. "And my ways are far beyond anything you could imagine. For just as the heavens are higher than the earth, so my ways are higher than your ways and my thoughts higher than your thoughts."

—ISAIAH 55:8-9

TODAY'S THOUGHT

Spiritual vision shows you a picture of the future that God has created for you. What do you see right now in the picture of your future? Is it filled with God? It's only when you empty yourself of your own plans and dreams for the future that God can fill you with his vision. It's only when you understand the extent of your sin, feel broken about it, rid yourself of it, and fill yourself with God that you will begin to see his picture of your future more clearly. Only then can you accomplish his work in your life and in the world.

TODAY'S PLAN

How can you see God's vision for your future?

PRAYER

TODAY'S PROMISE

The eyes of the Lord watch over those who do right, and his ears are open to their prayers. —1 PETER 3:12

TODAY'S THOUGHT

God not only listens carefully to every prayer, he also answers each one. God may answer yes, no, or wait, just as loving parents might answer the request of their child with one of these three responses. Answering yes to every request would spoil you and endanger your well-being. Answering no to every request would be vindictive, stingy, and hard on your spirit. Answering wait to every request would frustrate you. God always answers your prayers according to what he knows is best for you. Knowing that God always listens and answers should inspire you to pray continually, even if his answer is not always the one you wanted.

TODAY'S PLAN

How can you be more sensitive to recognizing the ways God answers each of your prayers?

APATHY

TODAY'S PROMISE

Anyone who isn't with me opposes me, and anyone who isn't working with me is actually working against me.

—MATTHEW 12:30

TODAY'S THOUGHT

Apathy can cause you to lose what you most value. If you are apathetic toward your wife, you are in danger of losing her. If you are apathetic about investing your money, you are in danger of losing your retirement income. If you are apathetic toward God, you are in danger of losing the priceless rewards that await his followers in heaven. Apathy often seems to be a passive force that simply lulls you to sleep, but it can also be an aggressive force that prevents you from keeping what is most meaningful and important.

TODAY'S PLAN

Are you in danger of losing something or someone dear to you? How can you protect yourself from the dangers of apathy?

PLANS

TODAY'S PROMISE

The LORD will work out his plans for my life.

—PSALM 138:8

TODAY'S THOUGHT

Planning demonstrates your desire to use your time wisely and makes you a good steward of the time and resources God has given you. So make your plans—but hold them loosely. You can be sure that God will give you new marching orders from time to time, and you must be ready and willing to adjust your own plans when that happens. God's plans for you are always the ones you want to be following.

TODAY'S PLAN

Are you ready to adjust your well-laid plans if God asks you to?

CHALLENGES

TODAY'S PROMISE

Dear brothers and sisters, when troubles come your way, consider it an opportunity for great joy. For you know that when your faith is tested, your endurance has a chance to grow. So let it grow, for when your endurance is fully developed, you will be perfect and complete, needing nothing. —JAMES 1:2-4

TODAY'S THOUGHT

Every day brings some kind of challenge. You may not rule a nation or run a large corporation, but you do face tough situations, difficult people, or subtle temptations. Some challenges God sends into your life; some he merely allows. Either way, they are often the tools God uses to help you develop spiritual strength and maturity. As you endure challenges today, you develop greater wisdom, integrity, and courage to face whatever will come your way tomorrow.

TODAY'S PLAN

What challenges are you facing right now? Can you envision how they might positively affect your life?

GOALS

TODAY'S PROMISE

Are you seeking great things for yourself? Don't do it!

—JEREMIAH 45:5

*If you want to be a friend of the world, you make
yourself an enemy of God.*

—JAMES 4:4

TODAY'S THOUGHT

The goals you set reflect what is most important
to you. When you set goals that benefit only
yourself, you do so at the cost of your relationship with God. When you set goals that are
pleasing to God, then you are truly pursuing the
greatest of rewards.

TODAY'S PLAN

*What are your personal goals? Evaluate the motivations
behind them and the rewards you seek to gain from them.
What spiritual goals can you set this week?*

CONTROL

TODAY'S PROMISE

For the LORD is God, and he created the heavens and earth and put everything in place. He made the world to be lived in, not to be a place of empty chaos. "I am the LORD," he says, "and there is no other."

—ISAIAH 45:18

TODAY'S THOUGHT

Sooner or later we all face situations beyond our control. But even when you find yourself in unpredictable, uncontrollable, frustrating circumstances, there is still one thing you can control: your reaction to the situation. You can trust God to work in your life and bring order, hope, and peace out of chaos.

TODAY'S PLAN

How would fully trusting in God's control affect your response to uncontrollable circumstances in your life?

ACKNOWLEDGMENT

TODAY'S PROMISE

*Everyone who acknowledges me publicly here on earth,
I will also acknowledge before my Father in heaven.*

—MATTHEW 10:32

TODAY'S THOUGHT

If you want Jesus Christ to acknowledge you
before God as one of his redeemed children, you
must acknowledge him before others as your
Savior and Redeemer. He will claim you on the
Day of Judgment according to whether or not
you claim him here on earth.

TODAY'S PLAN

*Do you acknowledge Jesus not only in your heart and mind but
also in public?*

CONVICTION

TODAY'S PROMISE

God has given both his promise and his oath. These two things are unchangeable because it is impossible for God to lie. Therefore, we who have fled to him for refuge can have great confidence as we hold to the hope that lies before us. —HEBREWS 6:18

TODAY'S THOUGHT

To effectively live out your faith, you must hold on to the conviction that God keeps his promises. When you trust God to do what he says he will do, you will have everything you need to live confidently for Christ because he promises to give it to you.

TODAY'S PLAN

Do you believe God will keep all his promises? Do you know what he has promised you?

DECISIONS

TODAY'S PROMISE

Your laws . . . give me wise advice. —PSALM 119:24

TODAY'S THOUGHT

Knowing the Bible and gleaning its wisdom gives you more options in your decision making and provides you with the discernment you need to make the best choices. A good decision is one that is consistent with the principles found in God's Word. If only one of the options you are deciding between would please God, then that is the right decision. If there are several options that are consistent with God's Word, then the process of trusting God to help you make the most of the path you choose may be more important than the decision itself.

TODAY'S PLAN

How can you look to the Bible for help with the decisions you're facing right now?

FOCUS

TODAY'S PROMISE

Pay attention to how you hear. To those who listen to my teaching, more understanding will be given. But for those who are not listening, even what they think they understand will be taken away from them.

—LUKE 8:18

TODAY'S THOUGHT

The words of Jesus demand our greatest focus because they have the authority of God; his teachings show us how to make the most out of life, both now and for eternity. Think of the most powerful, most influential person on earth. If that person were to talk to you, would you listen? Would you give him or her your full attention? Now think of the fact that Jesus is the Son of God—how much more should you give him your attention! When you focus on him, he promises you will understand his Word and his will.

TODAY'S PLAN

How much do you focus on the words of Jesus?

CHOICES

TODAY'S PROMISE

He guards the paths of the just and protects those who are faithful to him. Then you will understand what is right, just, and fair, and you will find the right way to go. For wisdom will enter your heart, and knowledge will fill you with joy.

—PROVERBS 2:8-10

TODAY'S THOUGHT

God has made his wisdom available to help you make appropriate choices. He shares his wisdom with you in many ways—through Jesus, the Holy Spirit, the Bible, your own conscience, and the godly advice of others. The closer you walk with God, the more wisdom you will have to make better choices. Immerse yourself in Scripture, prayer, and Christian fellowship, and you will find yourself knowing which choice is the right choice.

TODAY'S PLAN

God has made his wisdom available to you, but have you made yourself available to receive it? How can you draw closer to the God of wisdom?

PRODUCTIVITY

TODAY'S PROMISE

[Jesus said,] "I am the vine; you are the branches. Those who remain in me, and I in them, will produce much fruit. For apart from me you can do nothing. Anyone who does not remain in me is thrown away like a useless branch and withers." —JOHN 15:5-6

TODAY'S THOUGHT

Jesus taught that when a branch of a vine produces no fruit, it is useless—as good as dead. In the same way, a man whose life does not reflect the fruit of the Spirit is spiritually dead because his faith isn't strong enough to be lived out before others. If you truly believe the Good News about Jesus, it will affect your attitude and actions.

TODAY'S PLAN

Does your behavior reflect the presence of Jesus within you?

BOUNDARIES

TODAY'S PROMISE

Who are those who fear the LORD? He will show them the path they should choose. —PSALM 25:12

The path of the virtuous leads away from evil; whoever follows that path is safe. —PROVERBS 16:17

TODAY'S THOUGHT

When you're walking on an unfamiliar path in the woods, you need it to be clearly marked. If it's not, you could stray off and become hopelessly lost, exposing yourself to danger and fear. God's commands and laws clearly mark life's path before you. He provides you with the boundaries you need to avoid the dangers of getting lost.

TODAY'S PLAN

Have you been oblivious to any of God's path markers— the boundaries he gives you in the Bible? How can you stay within his boundaries?

LOYALTY

TODAY'S PROMISE

The LORD leads with unfailing love and faithfulness all who keep his covenant and obey his demands.

—PSALM 25:10

TODAY'S THOUGHT

When you have loyalty in a relationship, you know that relationship is secure and solid because it is built on trust. When you don't have loyalty or trust, you live in insecurity because you never know if you can count on that person. The Bible teaches that loyalty is part of God's character. He didn't just create loyalty—it is the essence of who he is. That is why he shows you unfailing love and faithfulness, no matter how much you disappoint him. God loves you no matter what—you can count on that. He leads those who are loyal to him in return. You can express your loyalty to God by obeying him.

TODAY'S PLAN

How secure is your relationship with God? How might increasing your loyalty improve your relationship with him?

ENDURANCE

TODAY'S PROMISE

I have fought the good fight, I have finished the race, and I have remained faithful. And now the prize awaits me—the crown of righteousness, which the Lord, the righteous Judge, will give me on the day of his return. And the prize is not just for me but for all who eagerly look forward to his appearing.

—2 TIMOTHY 4:7-8

TODAY'S THOUGHT

Just as marathoners must train hard to build up their endurance so they can run the race and finish well, so Christians must train hard to build endurance for living a life of faith in Jesus and staying strong to the end. When you have built up your endurance, you will not collapse during the race but will push on toward the goal of becoming more and more like Jesus. Then you will cross the finish line into heaven and receive the eternal rewards he has promised you.

TODAY'S PLAN

What are you doing to develop spiritual endurance?

CRISIS

TODAY'S PROMISE

[Jesus said,] "Here on earth you will have many trials and sorrows. But take heart, because I have overcome the world."

—JOHN 16:33

TODAY'S THOUGHT

Crisis should not surprise you. You should expect to encounter difficulties because we live in a fallen world. Jesus even tells us that we will have problems here on earth. His words of warning should keep you from panicking when crisis hits. And his promise of victory should keep you from becoming discouraged or feeling like there is no way out.

TODAY'S PLAN

Are you prepared for a crisis?

CHANGE

TODAY'S PROMISE

God is working in you, giving you the desire and the
power to do what pleases him. —PHILIPPIANS 2:13

TODAY'S THOUGHT

God doesn't force change on you. When you
invite him into your life, you give him permission to use his power to change you. If you try to
change on your own, you won't get good results,
but you will get discouraged. Instead, let the
very power of God himself begin a work of
transformation in you that will last a lifetime.
Your life will see dramatic changes if you allow
God to do his work in you.

TODAY'S PLAN

How can you allow God to change you from the
inside out?

BACKSLIDING

TODAY'S PROMISE

Everyone has sinned; we all fall short of God's glorious standard. Yet God, with undeserved kindness, declares that we are righteous. He did this through Christ Jesus when he freed us from the penalty for our sins.

—ROMANS 3:23-24

TODAY'S THOUGHT

It happens to everyone from time to time. You suddenly realize you're farther away from God than you should be, and you're worried. Backsliding often begins with simple neglect or falling back into a sinful habit. Only when you recognize what you've done can you confess it to God, and only by confessing your sin can you be forgiven and begin the process of restoring your relationship with him. God promises that when you take the time and effort to really listen to him, he will show you where you've strayed and bring you back to him.

TODAY'S PLAN

Are you further away from God than you want to be?

BUSYNESS

TODAY'S PROMISE

Jesus said, "Come to me, all of you who are weary and carry heavy burdens, and I will give you rest. Take my yoke upon you. Let me teach you, because I am humble and gentle at heart, and you will find rest for your souls."

—MATTHEW 11:28-29

TODAY'S THOUGHT

Too often we get caught up in the busyness of life. There are so many things to do, and before you know it, life is moving at break-neck speed. The faster you go, the harder it is to pay attention to the things right around you. Unfortunately, that means you end up speeding past so much of what is really important—God, family, friends. You must learn to slow down, to rest, to enjoy the blessings that are right in front of you. Jesus shows you how to slow down. He promises to give rest, refresh-ment, and meaning to your wearied and hurried soul.

TODAY'S PLAN

Are you so busy that you're racing by what's most important to you?

DISCIPLINE

TODAY'S PROMISE

To learn, you must love discipline; it is stupid to hate correction.   —PROVERBS 12:1

TODAY'S THOUGHT

Who in their right mind loves to be disciplined? Yet that is exactly the mind-set you must have if you want to learn from your mistakes and reach your God-given potential. Discipline is essential to developing skill, maturity, and character— there's no way around it. So learn to appreciate discipline, whether from God or from others, and you will learn more than you ever thought possible.

TODAY'S PLAN

How can you learn to enjoy the benefits of discipline?

FOLLOWING

TODAY'S PROMISE

Jesus spoke to the people once more and said, "I am the light of the world. If you follow me, you won't have to walk in darkness, because you will have the light that leads to life."

—JOHN 8:12

TODAY'S THOUGHT

God promises great rewards to those who follow him, not least of which is eternal life with him. If you want the light of Christ to shine in your life, you must follow where he leads. Following Jesus means staying close enough to him that you can always keep your eyes on him. When you keep your eyes on Jesus, you will be able to see which direction to go. He created you, he knows what's best for you, and he has prepared a place for you in eternity—doesn't it only make sense to follow him?

TODAY'S PLAN

Are you close enough to God to follow him as he leads you?

BLESSINGS

TODAY'S PROMISE

Blessed are those who trust in the LORD and have made the LORD their hope and confidence.

—JEREMIAH 17:7

TODAY'S THOUGHT

If you want God's blessings just so you can live an easier, more comfortable life, then you don't understand the nature of God's blessings. When you belong to the Lord, all that you are and all that you have is a gift from him, to be used by him to bless others. When you truly trust God, he promises you an abundance of blessings to be used to refresh others.

TODAY'S PLAN

How are you using the blessings God has given you to bless others?

HEALTH

TODAY'S PROMISE

All athletes are disciplined in their training. They do it to win a prize that will fade away, but we do it for an eternal prize.
                                        —1 CORINTHIANS 9:25

TODAY'S THOUGHT

Spiritual disciplines (such as prayer, Bible study, and worship) impact your physical life, and physical disciplines (such as exercise, good nutrition, and proper hygiene) influence your spiritual life too. Spiritual exercise should be as purposeful and strenuous as physical exercise. But remember that the benefits of spiritual fitness last for eternity, while the benefits of physical fitness last only as long as your body. Knowing the eternal benefits of spiritual exercise should motivate you to keep your physical and spiritual health in wholesome balance and help you experience a vibrant relationship with your Creator.

TODAY'S PLAN

Does your physical and spiritual health allow you to serve God to the best of your ability?

CONSISTENCY

TODAY'S PROMISE

We can be sure that we know him if we obey his commandments.

—1 JOHN 2:3

TODAY'S THOUGHT

God's rule for perfect living is to obey all of his commandments. But no one is perfect. That's why Jesus Christ died and rose again—to forgive your sins. The key, then, is to consistently try to obey God's commandments, realizing that you will sometimes fail. When you do fail, consistently seek Jesus and his forgiveness. Then you will be sure that you know him and belong to him.

TODAY'S PLAN

How consistently are you trying to obey God's commandments?

BROKENNESS

TODAY'S PROMISE

*My health may fail, and my spirit may grow weak,
but God remains the strength of my heart; he is mine
forever.*

—PSALM 73:26

TODAY'S THOUGHT

Brokenness makes you aware of your utter dependence on God. It breaks down your pride and self-
sufficiency. Brokenness often comes through
circumstances that overwhelm you or sin that
overtakes you. Those who accept and embrace
brokenness can have a greater influence on
others because of their vulnerability. You can be
sure that God will have a greater influence on you
when your brokenness becomes a channel for his
comfort, blessing, and help.

TODAY'S PLAN

*Do you need to experience brokenness in
order to experience a breakthrough with God?*

CALL OF GOD

TODAY'S PROMISE

God's gifts and his call can never be withdrawn.

—ROMANS 11:29

TODAY'S THOUGHT

God's call is like your family name. Even when you feel you've dishonored your family, you do not lose your name. The same principle applies when you are a member of God's family. Because you are his child, God has given you specific gifts and called you to do certain tasks for him. If you don't use the gifts God has given you, he won't take them away, but you will miss out on the best possible life he has planned for you. As long as you have life and breath, use your gifts to live out God's calling for your life—you can't lose.

TODAY'S PLAN

Do you feel like you've missed out on something God wanted you to do? How can you be ready to answer the next time he calls you?

AUTHORITY

TODAY'S PROMISE

Whoever wants to be a leader among you must be your servant. —MATTHEW 20:26

TODAY'S THOUGHT

If you want others to look up to you, then have a servant's heart, be willing to take responsibility for your actions instead of passing the buck when it's convenient, speak up when you see something that is wrong, and never seek glory for yourself. The world teaches people in authority to look and act in control, to step on the people under their authority, and to bend the rules instead of playing fair. But in the end, the people who have shown kindness, integrity, humility, and a deep love for God will be the most respected and honored.

TODAY'S PLAN

Are you living by God's definition of authority or by the world's?

CONSCIENCE

TODAY'S PROMISE

My conscience is clear, but that doesn't prove I'm right. It is the Lord himself who will examine me and decide.
—1 CORINTHIANS 4:4

TODAY'S THOUGHT

Always strive to maintain a clear conscience by being honest and trustworthy. This allows you to shrug off criticism that you know is unjustified. The most important thing is knowing that you answer to God above anyone else. If you are confident that God is pleased with your motives and actions, you can live with a clear conscience.

TODAY'S PLAN

Is your conscience clear enough that you handle criticism with confidence and grace?

GOOD-BYES

TODAY'S PROMISE

There is more than enough room in my Father's home. If this were not so, would I have told you that I am going to prepare a place for you? When everything is ready, I will come and get you, so that you will always be with me where I am. —JOHN 14:2-3

TODAY'S THOUGHT

Whether it's waving to your children each morning as they head off to school or grieving as you bury one of your parents, good-byes can be hard. Because of sin, farewells will always be a part of this life, but you will never have to say good-bye to God. No matter where you go, God is with you. He guides and comforts you as you—and your loved ones—come and go. How comforting to know that when you arrive in heaven, all the good-byes will be over and there will be only joyous greetings!

TODAY'S PLAN

Have you thought about the joy of never having to say good-bye in heaven?

FEBRUARY

PREPARATION

TODAY'S PROMISE

Anyone who listens to my teaching and follows it is wise, like a person who builds a house on solid rock.

—MATTHEW 7:24

TODAY'S THOUGHT

How can you make wise decisions at a moment's notice? The key is to be prepared by developing wisdom over time. You can't anticipate everything that might happen today, but when you are prepared spiritually—when you have developed godly wisdom—you will know the right thing to do so God can use you to accomplish good. You will be ready to act swiftly and decisively because you have a wellspring of wisdom to draw upon.

TODAY'S PLAN

Have you prepared yourself spiritually in the same way that you prepare in other areas of your life?

APOLOGY

TODAY'S PROMISE

Confess your sins to each other and pray for each other so that you may be healed. —JAMES 5:16

TODAY'S THOUGHT

Saying "I'm sorry" for something you have done wrong is one of the most difficult things to do. You have to recognize your fault, face it head-on, and then humble yourself enough to admit it to someone else. Offering a simple apology demonstrates that you are willing to open the door to healing and blessing. If you want to experience peace and growth in your relationships with loved ones, coworkers, or God himself, the practice of admitting you are wrong will help you reach a new level of trust and respect. The act of apologizing is also a powerful example to others.

TODAY'S PLAN

Is there someone you need to apologize to? How might your apology benefit both of you?

APPRECIATION

TODAY'S PROMISE

Give thanks to the LORD, for he is good! His faithful love endures forever. —1 CHRONICLES 16:34

TODAY'S THOUGHT

We often pray when we have a need. We often pray when we want something from God. But after God answers your prayer, do you remember to pray as often and as passionately in thanksgiving to him? When you understand God's awesome splendor, overwhelming power, and extravagant grace, you will be better able to appreciate the privilege of receiving his forgiveness and experiencing fellowship with him.

TODAY'S PLAN

How often do you thank God for answered prayer?

CHEATING

TODAY'S PROMISE

If you are faithful in little things, you will be faithful in large ones. But if you are dishonest in little things, you won't be honest with greater responsibilities. —LUKE 16:10

TODAY'S THOUGHT

Your character is tested in the small choices you make. Cheating in a little thing is cut out of the same piece of cloth as cheating in a big way. Just as a small drop of dye will color even a large glass of clear water, a small act of deception colors your whole character. God promises that when you are honest and faithful in small ways, he will give you more and greater opportunities to do good.

TODAY'S PLAN

Are you honest in even the smallest things?

SPIRITUAL WARFARE

TODAY'S PROMISE

The LORD is a warrior; Yahweh is his name!

—EXODUS 15:3

The LORD will march forth like a mighty hero; he will come out like a warrior, full of fury. He will shout his battle cry and crush all his enemies. —ISAIAH 42:13

TODAY'S THOUGHT

The goal of the forces of evil is to defy God and to wear down believers until they are led into sin. A battle rages in the spiritual realm, and as a believer, you are right in the thick of it. But God himself is a warrior. God is always ready to fight on your behalf, to come to your defense, to provide you with armor so that you can fight alongside him (see Ephesians 6:11-18). Without the Lord fighting with you, you would be helpless to withstand the enemy. But if you join God in battle, you are guaranteed the victory!

TODAY'S PLAN

How can you join God in fighting the spiritual battle going on around you?

DISCOURAGEMENT

TODAY'S PROMISE

Do not be afraid! Don't be discouraged by this mighty army, for the battle is not yours, but God's. . . . Do not be afraid or discouraged. Go out against them. . . . for the LORD is with you!

—2 CHRONICLES 20:15-17

TODAY'S THOUGHT

The people of Judah could see only a vast enemy army, not their God standing by to destroy it. It's easy to focus on your problems and forget that God is near and ready to help. Be careful to separate your feelings of discouragement from the facts of reality: You have the assurance of God's love for you. Discouragement can cause you to doubt God's love, drawing you away from the source of your greatest help. Realize that God will fight on your behalf and help you succeed when you see that he is right beside you.

TODAY'S PLAN

Are you getting discouraged trying to overcome life's challenges all by yourself? Why don't you let God help?

EMPTINESS

TODAY'S PROMISE

He saved us, not because of the righteous things we had done, but because of his mercy. He washed away our sins, giving us a new birth and new life through the Holy Spirit. He generously poured out the Spirit upon us through Jesus Christ our Savior.

—TITUS 3:5-6

TODAY'S THOUGHT

Everyone is searching for something to fill the emptiness in their souls. But too many people try to fill their lives with the wrong things. The key is to fill yourself with something that will last. God promises that when you accept the gift of salvation and believe in Jesus Christ as Savior, you are filled with his Holy Spirit. The presence of God is within you, and you receive his love, help, encouragement, peace, and comfort.

TODAY'S PLAN

Are you allowing God to fill the emptiness in your heart?

HOLINESS

TODAY'S PROMISE

May he . . . make your hearts strong, blameless, and holy as you stand before God our Father when our Lord Jesus comes again with all his holy people.

—1 THESSALONIANS 3:13

TODAY'S THOUGHT

There is no way that you can ever live a perfectly holy life by your own efforts. It is only through your faith in Christ's death on the cross that you become holy in God's eyes. He took on the punishment that you deserve. When you accept Jesus as Lord of your life and confess your sins to him, his forgiveness cleanses you. This doesn't mean you no longer sin, but God actually looks at you as though you are blameless and holy.

TODAY'S PLAN

Does God see you as holy, or do you still need to experience God's forgiveness?

REPUTATION

TODAY'S PROMISE

Never let loyalty and kindness leave you! Tie them around your neck as a reminder. Write them deep within your heart. Then you will find favor with both God and people, and you will earn a good reputation.
—PROVERBS 3:3-4

TODAY'S THOUGHT

Everyone has a reputation. Whether you intentionally try to project a certain image or you couldn't care less what others think, people still form an opinion of you based on your personality, your character, your behavior, and your abilities. A good reputation can help you make friends and gain respect. A bad reputation can attract others of ill repute to you, or it can leave you isolated, shunned, and disrespected. God promises you will earn a good reputation when you show kindness, loyalty, and love to your neighbors.

TODAY'S PLAN

What kind of reputation are you building?

ADVICE

TODAY'S PROMISE

Listen to my instruction and be wise. Don't ignore it.

—PROVERBS 8:33

TODAY'S THOUGHT

The key to getting great advice is being open to it. It is easy to ignore good advice when you think you already know what to do or how to do it. Being open-minded will prepare you to receive, evaluate, and follow good advice. Then your understanding and wisdom will increase, and you will learn something from each situation that will help you in the future.

TODAY'S PLAN

When was the last time you listened to good advice? How can you be more open to it?

BOREDOM

TODAY'S PROMISE

Our great desire is that you will keep on loving others as long as life lasts, in order to make certain that what you hope for will come true. Then you will not become spiritually dull and indifferent.	—HEBREWS 6:11-12

TODAY'S THOUGHT

Being a Christian might seem boring to many people—"Don't do this," "You can't do that." But those who understand what the Christian life is all about find it full and exciting. When you realize that almighty God wants to work through you to accomplish his work in the world, you will be amazed to see the wonderful opportunities he puts before you. If you become bored in your Christian life, try making yourself available to God and asking him to pour out his blessings through you to others.

TODAY'S PLAN

Do you believe that God wants to work through you to accomplish great things? If you believe this and act on it, you will never be bored.

INTIMACY

TODAY'S PROMISE

Learn to know . . . God . . . intimately. Worship and serve him with your whole heart and a willing mind. For the LORD sees every heart and knows every plan and thought. If you seek him, you will find him.

— 1 CHRONICLES 28:9

TODAY'S THOUGHT

We often resist being vulnerable with God because of our sins, especially the ones we don't really want to give up. But intimacy requires full disclosure, not hiding or covering up. When you confess your sins to God, ask for forgiveness, and commit yourself to loving him with your whole heart and mind, your relationship with him is restored, and you will know him in the deepest possible way. He promises that if you look for him, you will find him.

TODAY'S PLAN

Has it been awhile since you've enjoyed intimacy in your relationship with God? How can you become more vulnerable in his presence?

FAITHFULNESS

TODAY'S PROMISE

If we are unfaithful, he remains faithful, for he cannot deny who he is.
                                                          —2 TIMOTHY 2:13

TODAY'S THOUGHT

Who are you really, deep down inside? Do you really love others? Are you really faithful to your family, friends, and coworkers? Faithfulness is necessary to maintain love because even those closest to you will disappoint you at times. But God loves you and remains faithful to you even when you disappoint him with your sin and rebellion. Model that same love to others, and remain faithful to them even when they fail you. Then you will show your love to be genuine, and others will know that you truly care.

TODAY'S PLAN

Are you passing the test of faithfulness?

LOVE

TODAY'S PROMISE

Hatred stirs up quarrels, but love makes up for all offenses. —PROVERBS 10:12

Love is patient and kind. Love is not jealous or boastful or proud or rude. It does not demand its own way. It is not irritable, and it keeps no record of being wronged. —1 CORINTHIANS 13:4-5

TODAY'S THOUGHT

Unconditional love means loving someone and doing the right thing even when the person you love hurts you. God shows us unconditional love, but consistently demonstrating that kind of love to others is perhaps the hardest thing for human beings to do. Unconditional love is the only way to experience meaningful and fulfilling relationships, and it is the only way to win over someone's heart.

TODAY'S PLAN

Who needs to receive unconditional love from you? How can you learn to show others the same love God has shown you?

TITHING

TODAY'S PROMISE

"Bring all the tithes into the storehouse so there will be enough food in my Temple. If you do," says the LORD of Heaven's Armies, "I will open the windows of heaven for you. I will pour out a blessing so great you won't have enough room to take it in! Try it! Put me to the test!"
—MALACHI 3:10

TODAY'S THOUGHT

Tithing is one way God meets the needs of his people. When you tithe, you show your commitment to God and his work, help those in need, and honor God for his provision and faithfulness. You keep God at the top of your priority list and gain the proper perspective on the rest of your paycheck. Instead of asking, "How much of my money do I need to give to God?" ask yourself, "How much of God's money do I need to keep?" As you meet the needs of others, God will graciously meet—and exceed—your own.

TODAY'S PLAN

Do you need to develop the discipline of tithing?

PERFECTION

TODAY'S PROMISE

I don't mean to say that I have already achieved these things or that I have already reached perfection. But I press on to possess that perfection for which Christ Jesus first possessed me. —PHILIPPIANS 3:12

TODAY'S THOUGHT

Many of us strive for perfection in our lives. We want to be the perfect husband or father, perform flawlessly on the job, or be supremely skilled at a sport or hobby. But on earth we will always be struggling against the reality of our humanness and sinful nature, which stand in the way of our quest for perfection. What we are really longing for is heaven, where perfection is the norm. Jesus is perfect, holy, and blameless. Through his death on the cross, he exchanges our human sinfulness for his perfect holiness and promises that one day we will be perfect in heaven.

TODAY'S PLAN

How can you take comfort today from the promise of perfection in heaven?

DOUBT

TODAY'S PROMISE

When doubts filled my mind, your comfort gave me renewed hope and cheer.　　　　　—PSALM 94:19

TODAY'S THOUGHT

Virtually every biblical hero struggled with doubts about God or God's ability or desire to help. God doesn't mind when you doubt as long as you continue to seek him in the midst of it. Doubt can become sin if it leads you away from God and into skepticism, cynicism, or hard-heartedness. But God promises that doubt can become a blessing if your honest searching leads you to a better understanding of God and a deeper faith in him. When others see your hope in God even as you struggle with doubt, they will be inspired to follow your example and cling to their faith, no matter what their circumstances.

TODAY'S PLAN

When you find yourself doubting God, do you let it move you closer to him or farther away?

INVESTMENTS

TODAY'S PROMISE

Give, and you will receive. Your gift will return to you in full—pressed down, shaken together to make room for more, running over, and poured into your lap. The amount you give will determine the amount you get back.

—LUKE 6:38

TODAY'S THOUGHT

One of the unique promises of the Bible is that the more you give, the more you receive—not necessarily in material possessions, but in spiritual and eternal rewards. This is a truth that can only be learned by doing. Your monetary investments will become worthless to you when you die—you can't take them with you. But any spiritual investments you make will impact you for eternity.

TODAY'S PLAN

What are some ways you can increase your spiritual investments?

GIVING UP

TODAY'S PROMISE

*Though I fall, I will rise again. Though I sit in
darkness, the LORD will be my light.* —MICAH 7:8

TODAY'S THOUGHT

When you fail, you must get up again. Many
inspiring success stories are about people who
failed many times but never gave up. Most important is your relationship with God. If you don't
give up on him, he promises you the ultimate
victory of eternal life with him in the perfect
world of heaven.

TODAY'S PLAN

Have you ever been tempted to give up on God?

AGING

TODAY'S PROMISE

I will be your God throughout your lifetime—until your hair is white with age. I made you, and I will care for you. I will carry you along and save you.

—ISAIAH 46:4

TODAY'S THOUGHT

God's love will last for all of your days on earth and into eternity. This promise gives you a profound picture of God's care. He walks alongside you, and he will carry you when you can no longer walk. In the end, he will bring you through death to your final, glorious destination.

TODAY'S PLAN

Are you aging gracefully, secure in God's ever-present care for you?

GENEROSITY

TODAY'S PROMISE

Remember this—a farmer who plants only a few seeds will get a small crop. But the one who plants generously will get a generous crop. —2 CORINTHIANS 9:6

TODAY'S THOUGHT

You should not give in order to grow richer, but your resources will grow when you give more. What you receive in return may be spiritual or relational rather than material. One of the great paradoxes of the Christian life is that the more generously you give, the more God blesses you in some way. One of the reasons for this is that the same qualities that make you responsible and trustworthy also make you generous. But the primary reason is that God in his grace entrusts more to you so that you can be a greater channel for bringing his blessings into this world.

TODAY'S PLAN

How generous are you with the resources God has given you?

STUBBORNNESS

TODAY'S PROMISE

Be careful then. . . . Make sure that your own hearts are not evil and unbelieving, turning you away from the living God. You must warn each other every day, while it is still "today," so that none of you will be deceived by sin and hardened against God. For if we are faithful to the end, trusting God just as firmly as when we first believed, we will share in all that belongs to Christ. —HEBREWS 3:12-14

TODAY'S THOUGHT

Has your heart become hard and stubborn, or do you reach out to God whatever your circumstances? When you cut yourself off from God, you cut off your lifeline to the only One who can really help you. A stubborn heart rejects the only thing that can save—God's love. A tender heart seeks God's help and notices his perfectly timed responses.

TODAY'S PLAN

What is the condition of your heart?

IMPATIENCE

TODAY'S PROMISE

Haste makes mistakes. People ruin their lives by their own foolishness and then are angry at the LORD.

—PROVERBS 19:2-3

TODAY'S THOUGHT

Impatience is an enemy of faith. Waiting on the Lord means having the patience and self-control to trust that God's timing is best. Most goals are accomplished through many small steps over a long period of time. You are most likely to make mistakes when you begin to get impatient to accomplish a particular goal. When you look too far ahead in your desire to get results right now, you overlook the smaller steps that get you to your goal, which causes you to stumble.

Trust in God, and avoid the mistakes of so many others.

TODAY'S PLAN

Are you becoming impatient to reach a certain goal?

POWER

TODAY'S PROMISE

Jesus came and told his disciples, "I have been given all authority in heaven and on earth. Therefore, go and make disciples of all the nations, baptizing them in the name of the Father and the Son and the Holy Spirit. Teach these new disciples to obey all the commands I have given you. And be sure of this: I am with you always, even to the end of the age."

—MATTHEW 28:18-20

TODAY'S THOUGHT

Jesus has complete authority over all the earth and all spiritual powers, and he has promised to exercise it on your behalf. As you serve him, you have the promise of his presence as well as the promise of his power.

TODAY'S PLAN

Are you giving Jesus the opportunity to exercise his power in your life? Do you know someone who needs to know the power of Jesus?

BIBLE

TODAY'S PROMISE

The message is very close at hand; it is on your lips and in your heart so that you can obey it.

—DEUTERONOMY 30:14

TODAY'S THOUGHT

What you fill your heart and mind with is what you become. Memorizing Scripture puts God's Word at your fingertips and allows you to meditate on his life-changing message at any time. You will have God's guidance available to you in all times and all situations when you keep God's Word in your heart and mind.

TODAY'S PLAN

Have you filled your heart and mind with God's Word?

SUCCESS

TODAY'S PROMISE

But the LORD said to Samuel, "Don't judge by his appearance or height. . . . The LORD doesn't see things the way you see them. People judge by outward appearance, but the LORD looks at the heart."

—1 SAMUEL 16:7

TODAY'S THOUGHT

God's standards of success differ greatly from our own. He measures success by faithfulness, not by quantities or results. It is a spiritual rather than a numerical value. Too often we measure success in terms of appearances and external qualities, but God looks at the heart. He promises to judge your success according to your motives, devotion, and commitment to him, not according to any prestige, possessions, or power you may have.

TODAY'S PLAN

Does God consider you a success?

TEMPTATION

TODAY'S PROMISE

You have heard the commandment that says, "You must not commit adultery." But I say, anyone who even looks at a woman with lust has already committed adultery with her in his heart. —MATTHEW 5:27-28

TODAY'S THOUGHT

Temptation often begins with the eyes and travels quickly to the heart. What you do immediately after you see something or someone that poses a temptation for you will affect your thoughts and actions beyond the situation at hand. If you let your eyes linger where they shouldn't, your mind will follow and will find ways to justify your gaze. Then your heart will start tugging you in that direction. The first step in avoiding temptation is taking your eyes off whatever may be tempting you.

TODAY'S PLAN

How can you protect your eyes from whatever tempts you?

WEAKNESSES

TODAY'S PROMISE

Yes, I am the vine; you are the branches. Those who remain in me, and I in them, will produce much fruit. For apart from me you can do nothing. —JOHN 15:5

TODAY'S THOUGHT

Faith that is placed in your own strength or in other people or things becomes weak because it is detached from the greatest source of strength—God. Stay connected to God, who supplies you with supernatural strength. Let his strength work through your weaknesses to produce spiritual fruit for him.

TODAY'S PLAN

Are you trying to do something on your own, without God's help? How might this make you spiritually weak?

RESTORATION

TODAY'S PROMISE

Do not banish me from your presence, and don't take your Holy Spirit from me. Restore to me the joy of your salvation, and make me willing to obey you. Then I will teach your ways to rebels, and they will return to you. . . . You do not desire a sacrifice, or I would offer one. . . . The sacrifice you desire is a broken spirit. You will not reject a broken and repentant heart, O God. —PSALM 51:11-13, 16-17

TODAY'S THOUGHT

God's grace is greater than your failure. No matter how often you fail, God welcomes you back. Satan wins when he keeps you from turning back to God. Restoration begins when you return to God. He will not despise your broken and repentant heart; in fact, he knows that is the only way you can be restored to him. He promises to forgive you, help you start over, and give you joy.

TODAY'S PLAN

Do you need to return to God? What's holding you back?

MARCH

VULNERABILITY

TODAY'S PROMISE

The word of God is alive and powerful. . . . It exposes our innermost thoughts and desires. Nothing in all creation is hidden from God. Everything is naked and exposed before his eyes, and he is the one to whom we are accountable. —HEBREWS 4:12-13

TODAY'S THOUGHT

You must be completely vulnerable to God's work in you to make you everything he created you to be. If you hold back from God, you can't reach your God-given potential. Confess your sin, seek God's forgiveness, and commit yourself to living his way. The more vulnerable you are before God, the more he releases you from a life of regret and guilt. You have nothing to fear, because God already knows you and still loves you.

TODAY'S PLAN

Have you allowed yourself to be completely vulnerable with God?

STRENGTH

TODAY'S PROMISE

I pray that from his glorious, unlimited resources he will empower you with inner strength through his Spirit. . . . Then you will be made complete with all the fullness of life and power that comes from God.

—EPHESIANS 3:16, 19

TODAY'S THOUGHT

A weightlifter's strength is determined by the number of pounds he can lift. The strength of a building is measured by its resistance to external forces that threaten its stability. The strength of a corporation is often defined by its net assets. But what about spiritual strength? The Bible teaches that spiritual strength gives you the power to bear burdens, a foundation to resist the pressures of temptation, the faith to move mountains, and the assurance of salvation and eternal life.

TODAY'S PLAN

How great is your spiritual strength?

AMBITION

TODAY'S PROMISE

[Jesus said,] "If any of you wants to be my follower, you must turn from your selfish ways, take up your cross, and follow me. If you try to hang on to your life, you will lose it. But if you give up your life for my sake and for the sake of the Good News, you will save it. And what do you benefit if you gain the whole world but lose your own soul?"

—MARK 8:34-36

TODAY'S THOUGHT

There's a difference between wanting to be a part of God's great work and wanting personal greatness through God's work. It's the difference between desiring to serve God and using God to serve yourself. Human ambition can fool you into striving for everything you desire in this world at the cost of losing your reward in heaven. God promises that the ambition to be a part of his great work will help you discover meaning in your life, as well as eternal life and heavenly rewards.

TODAY'S PLAN

What is the source of your ambition?

ANGER

TODAY'S PROMISE

*Stop being angry! Turn from your rage! Do not lose
your temper—it only leads to harm.* —PSALM 37:8

TODAY'S THOUGHT

Anger is often a reaction to your pride being
hurt. When you are confronted, rejected,
ignored, or don't get your own way, anger acts
as a defense mechanism to protect your ego. It is
common to feel angry when someone confronts
you about your own sinful actions because
you don't want others to think you have done
something wrong. But the Bible promises that
anger—unless it is righteous anger—will always
bring harm.

TODAY'S PLAN

What kinds of things tend to make you angry?

GOOD DEEDS

TODAY'S PROMISE

Faith by itself isn't enough. Unless it produces good deeds, it is dead and useless. . . . Can't you see that faith without good deeds is useless? —JAMES 2:17, 20

TODAY'S THOUGHT

Simply doing good deeds for others doesn't mean you have faith in God; but when you have faith in God, your heart is so full of love and compassion for others that it spills out in the form of good deeds. Those who have genuine faith in God always bear the fruit of good works in their lives. They praise and thank God, tell others of his goodness, and rely on him for help. When God is first in your life, you will be amazed at what he will do through you.

TODAY'S PLAN

Does your faith in God spill out of your heart in the form of good deeds?

VICTORY

TODAY'S PROMISE

Every child of God defeats this evil world, and we achieve this victory through our faith. And who can win this battle against the world? Only those who believe that Jesus is the Son of God. —1 JOHN 5:4-5

TODAY'S THOUGHT

Your first line of defense against spiritual attack is to draw strength from God, who is more powerful than your problems or your enemies. Your faith in God is a shield that protects you from the evils you face every day. Without strong faith, you would easily be defeated in the battle against sin and Satan. Even when life seems overwhelming, hold tightly to your faith, and you will withstand the attacks against you. And rejoice—you know that God has already won the victory!

TODAY'S PLAN

How can you live differently knowing that God has won the victory?

JUSTICE

TODAY'S PROMISE

Be just and fair to all. Do what is right and good, for I am coming soon to rescue you and to display my righteousness among you. Blessed are all those who are careful to do this.

—ISAIAH 56:1-2

TODAY'S THOUGHT

Justice is important because it ensures fairness, equality, consistency, and equal opportunity to all. True justice eliminates politics, double standards, inequity, and oppression. Justice comes from the heart of God, which is why God blesses people who are just. If you insist on justice, fairness, and equity in the way you deal with others, you will experience blessing from God.

TODAY'S PLAN

Is justice an essential part of your life?

MONEY

TODAY'S PROMISE

[The LORD] did all this so you would never say to yourself, "I have achieved this wealth with my own strength and energy." Remember the LORD your God. He is the one who gives you power to be successful. —DEUTERONOMY 8:17-18

TODAY'S THOUGHT

Some people say wealth is sinful. But money is not inherently good or bad. What you do with your money, however, has the potential to be good, bad, or simply useless in the eyes of God. Without the financial support of Christians who have been blessed with wealth, many good ministries would have to shut their doors. But God also tells us there is danger in acquiring money. Always remember that your money is a gift from God, and strive to be grateful and responsible with whatever he gives you.

TODAY'S PLAN

What are you doing with the money God has given you? Is it good, bad, or useless?

PERSEVERANCE

TODAY'S PROMISE

Because the Sovereign LORD helps me, I will not be disgraced. Therefore, I have set my face like a stone, determined to do his will. And I know that I will not be put to shame.

—ISAIAH 50:7

TODAY'S THOUGHT

Your ability to persevere is based on the promise of God's persistent, faithful work in your life. God never stops working in you, and that should motivate you to persevere through life. The fuel you need to accomplish this is the power of God working in you. As you become more in tune with God, God's power will strengthen you and ignite your ability to persevere—not just to endure, but to persevere with joy!

TODAY'S PLAN

What can you do to develop perseverance?

TRUST

TODAY'S PROMISE

Trust in the LORD with all your heart; do not depend on your own understanding. Seek his will in all you do, and he will show you which path to take.

—PROVERBS 3:5-6

TODAY'S THOUGHT

Trusting God with all your heart means resolving to let him show you how to live and to obey his Word in all areas of your life. As a human being with a sinful nature, you will never be able to completely achieve this goal, but that should not stop you from doing your best. When you trust him and seek his will, God promises to direct you to people, places, and opportunities that will give your life purpose and satisfaction.

TODAY'S PLAN

Are you trusting God with your whole heart?

CHANGE

TODAY'S PROMISE

If you confess with your mouth that Jesus is Lord and believe in your heart that God raised him from the dead, you will be saved.

—ROMANS 10:9

This means that anyone who belongs to Christ has become a new person. The old life is gone; a new life has begun!

—2 CORINTHIANS 5:17

TODAY'S THOUGHT

If you are truly sorry for your sins and confess them to God, and if you believe that God's Son, Jesus, died on the cross to take the punishment for sin that you deserve, then God forgives you and grants you salvation. The moment you are saved, the Holy Spirit enters your life and begins transforming you into a new person from the inside out. Your life will be forever changed!

TODAY'S PLAN

Can others see that God has changed you?

ENEMIES

TODAY'S PROMISE

All of you should be of one mind. Sympathize with each other. Love each other as brothers and sisters. Be tenderhearted, and keep a humble attitude. Don't repay evil for evil. Don't retaliate with insults when people insult you. Instead, pay them back with a blessing. That is what God has called you to do, and he will bless you for it. —1 PETER 3:8-9

TODAY'S THOUGHT

Showing love to your enemies seems completely unreasonable—unless you realize that you were an enemy of God until he forgave you. When you love your enemies, you see them as Christ does—people in need of grace and forgiveness. Getting to that point takes prayer. When you pray for those people, you can't help but feel compassion for them. When you respond with prayer and blessing instead of retaliation when someone hurts you, God promises to bless you. God can even turn enemies into friends.

TODAY'S PLAN

How can you show love to your enemies?

CONTENTMENT

TODAY'S PROMISE

By his divine power, God has given us everything we need for living a godly life. We have received all of this by coming to know him, the one who called us to himself by means of his marvelous glory and excellence.

—2 PETER 1:3

TODAY'S THOUGHT

When your contentment depends on things going your way, you will become unhappy when they don't. When your contentment comes from watching Jesus meet your needs, you will be secure and happy because you will have all you need. You will know that God's plan for you, which is always best, is working out. He will teach you to discern the valuable things in life from the distractions.

TODAY'S PLAN

How can you learn to find greater contentment in the things God has already given you?

STRENGTH

TODAY'S PROMISE

I love you, LORD; you are my strength. The LORD is my rock, my fortress, and my savior; my God is my rock, in whom I find protection. He is my shield, the power that saves me, and my place of safety. . . . In your strength I can crush an army; with my God I can scale any wall. —PSALM 18:1-2, 29

TODAY'S THOUGHT

God's strength gives you the power to do things you could never do on your own. You can withstand the toughest attacks and even take the offensive in overcoming challenges. You can live without fear because you can rely on God's rock-solid love and salvation. He promises to use his strength to protect you and help you do the impossible.

TODAY'S PLAN

Do you feel like you need more strength? Do you have the courage to ask God for his strength?

UNDERSTANDING

TODAY'S PROMISE

This same Good News that came to you is going out all over the world. It is bearing fruit everywhere by changing lives, just as it changed your lives from the day you first heard and understood the truth about God's wonderful grace. —COLOSSIANS 1:6

TODAY'S THOUGHT

Anyone who's tried to communicate with someone who speaks a different language knows how big the gap can be between hearing words and understanding their meaning. Understanding can be described as knowledge that is made intimate and personal. The Bible emphasizes that you can not only know spiritual truths as facts and doctrine, but you can understand them—in other words, you can have an intimate and personal relationship with almighty God, and that will transform your life.

TODAY'S PLAN

Have you ever considered the difference between knowing about God and understanding him on a personal level?

MOTIVATION

Mark out a straight path for your feet so that those who are weak and lame will not fall but become strong.

—HEBREWS 12:13

If you lack motivation in your spiritual walk, perhaps your self-imposed expectations are too high. God understands that growth takes time. Set smaller goals for yourself, goals that are challenging yet attainable. Develop a quantifiable method of determining when that goal has been met. As you meet these smaller goals, you will be more motivated to keep moving toward your bigger goals. You will be more confident as you grow stronger in your faith. Then as you display steady progress in your walk with Christ, you will motivate others in their faith walk as well.

What are some small, attainable goals you can set for yourself in your spiritual growth?

ACCOMPLISHMENTS

TODAY'S PROMISE

You didn't choose me. I chose you. I appointed you to go and produce lasting fruit. —JOHN 15:16

Tell them to use their money to do good. They should be rich in good works and generous to those in need, always being ready to share with others. By doing this they will be storing up their treasure as a good foundation for the future so that they may experience true life. —1 TIMOTHY 6:18-19

TODAY'S THOUGHT

Most of your earthly accomplishments don't last forever and are even soon forgotten. Thankfully, God's love is not based on your achievements but on his own choice to love and cherish you. The kinds of accomplishments that last are those that are done for rewards in heaven, not on earth.

TODAY'S PLAN

Are you working toward any accomplishments that will bring you greater rewards in heaven than on earth?

LISTENING

TODAY'S PROMISE

And so, my children, listen to me, for all who follow my ways are joyful.
—PROVERBS 8:32

TODAY'S THOUGHT

Just as a piano is tuned using a standard tuning fork, so you can only get in tune with God by comparing yourself to the unchanging standards for living found in the Bible. As God communicates to you through his Word, you will begin to hear or discern just what he wants of you. As your spiritual hearing is fine-tuned, you will become a better listener, better able to hear God when he calls you to a certain task that he has reserved just for you. There is nothing that brings greater joy than being in tune with God!

TODAY'S PLAN

Would God say you are a good listener?

CONSCIENCE

TODAY'S PROMISE

Cling to your faith in Christ, and keep your conscience clear. For some people have deliberately violated their consciences; as a result, their faith has been shipwrecked.

—1 TIMOTHY 1:19

TODAY'S THOUGHT

Your conscience helps you know whether you are living in line with God's will. It is one of the gifts God gives you to keep you sensitive to his moral code. But you must use this gift and take good care of it. If you don't listen to and obey your conscience, it will become harder and harder to hear it. It can even malfunction. If your conscience is working faithfully, it will help you know the difference between right and wrong. Let God sharpen your conscience and speak to you through his holy Word.

TODAY'S PLAN

Are you having trouble determining what is right? How can you resensitize your conscience?

FEAR OF GOD

TODAY'S PROMISE

Fear of the LORD is the foundation of wisdom.

—PROVERBS 9:10

How joyful are those who fear the LORD—all who follow his ways!

—PSALM 128:1

TODAY'S THOUGHT

To fear the Lord is to recognize that he is holy, almighty, righteous, all-knowing, and wise. When you have the proper understanding of God, you also gain a clearer picture of yourself as sinful, weak, and needy. The only fitting response to the God of the universe, who loves you despite your failures, is to fall at his feet in humble awe. When you fear the Lord by displaying this attitude of humility and reverence, he promises to give you wisdom and joy.

TODAY'S PLAN

What might you gain from developing a proper fear of God?

THOUGHTS

TODAY'S PROMISE

It is what comes from inside that defiles you. . . .
All these vile things come from within; they are what
defile you.
— MARK 7:20, 23

I know, my God, that you examine our hearts and
rejoice when you find integrity there.
— 1 CHRONICLES 29:17

TODAY'S THOUGHT

Controlling our thoughts is perhaps one of
the greatest struggles men face. God takes your
thought life seriously because your thoughts
reflect the condition of your heart. Even if you
do not immediately act on your thoughts, they
do shape your attitudes and, eventually, your
actions. When bad thoughts pop into your
mind, immediately redirect them by praying or meditating on Scripture. This takes
discipline, but it is an effective and godly way
to manage your thoughts.

TODAY'S PLAN

What kind of thoughts will be reflected by your actions
today?

SUCCESS

TODAY'S PROMISE

Study this Book of Instruction continually. Meditate on it day and night so you will be sure to obey everything written in it. Only then will you prosper and succeed in all you do.

—JOSHUA 1:8

TODAY'S THOUGHT

The Bible teaches that you will be successful in your life when you commit to vigorous spiritual training. This should include meditating on God's Word and inviting God to be part of your life, as well as consistently obeying God's commands. Then you will gain victory over your fears, over Satan's attempts to derail your relationship with God, and ultimately over sin and death. God promises that you will experience success and joy.

TODAY'S PLAN

Are you prepared for the training that is required to be spiritually successful?

SPIRITUAL WARFARE

TODAY'S PROMISE

The devil . . . was a murderer from the beginning. He has always hated the truth, because there is no truth in him. When he lies, it is consistent with his character; for he is a liar and the father of lies. —JOHN 8:44

TODAY'S THOUGHT

Satan is determined to destroy your faith by leading you into sin and discouragement. He attacks you with blatant temptations and subtle deceptions. The Bible is your field manual for fighting back. It trains you in using the best weapons and tactics for this very real and dangerous battle. Because Scripture is so essential, Satan's first plan of action is often to distort God's Word. If he can compromise your belief in the Bible, he can get you to question God's will for you. Study the Bible so you know it well enough to recognize Satan's lies. Then you will be able to fight his lies with God's truth.

TODAY'S PLAN

Are you able to recognize when Satan is using the tactic of distorting God's Word?

USED BY GOD

TODAY'S PROMISE

If you keep yourself pure, you will be a special utensil for honorable use. Your life will be clean, and you will be ready for the Master to use you for every good work.

—2 TIMOTHY 2:21

TODAY'S THOUGHT

God does holy work through unholy people because no human being is perfect. He will use you if you ask him to cleanse you and make you pure, even though he knows you are not perfect on your own. The key to being used by God is not perfection but a willingness to serve him, to ask for forgiveness when you need it, to live humbly, to try to obey him. This shows that you are ready for God to use you, and he promises to increase your purpose and fulfillment as well as accomplish good things through you.

TODAY'S PLAN

Are you willing to be used by God despite your imperfections?

APPROVAL

TODAY'S PROMISE

Well done, my good and faithful servant. You have been faithful in handling this small amount, so now I will give you many more responsibilities.

—MATTHEW 25:23

TODAY'S THOUGHT

Those who consistently do a good job can usually be trusted with more freedom and responsibility. Their work receives approval from someone who supervises or oversees them. In the same way, the more you serve God, the more he will reward your faithfulness and give you opportunities to serve him with greater freedom and responsibility. Remember that God's love for you never changes, but his approval of your work is based on how well you serve him.

TODAY'S PLAN

Does God approve of you enough to give you greater responsibility in serving him?

ATTITUDE

TODAY'S PROMISE

So, my dear brothers and sisters, be strong and immovable. Always work enthusiastically for the Lord, for you know that nothing you do for the Lord is ever useless. —1 CORINTHIANS 15:58

TODAY'S THOUGHT

Attitude is important because it affects your thoughts, motives, and actions. As a believer, you can maintain a positive attitude that is based on the fact that the God of the universe created you, loves you, and promises you salvation and eternal life. God is working for you, not against you. Remind yourself of these truths every day. It will positively affect your attitude, which will positively affect the way you live and serve God.

TODAY'S PLAN

On a scale of one to ten, how is your attitude? How can you bring it up a few notches today?

VALUES

TODAY'S PROMISE

Who may worship in your sanctuary, LORD? Who may enter your presence on your holy hill? Those who lead blameless lives and do what is right, speaking the truth from sincere hearts.

—PSALM 15:1-2

TODAY'S THOUGHT

Have you ever heard someone say, "He doesn't have any values"? Such a statement is simply not true. Everyone has values, either good or bad. And your values are clear to those around you because what you do, how you spend your time and money, and what you talk about show exactly what you value the most. This is even true of God—what he does and says shows what he values most. For example, God made you in his own image, so he must value you! He values you so much that he sent his own Son to die for you so that you can come into his presence.

TODAY'S PLAN

Does your life show that your values are the same as God's?

PLANS

TODAY'S PROMISE

He renews my strength. He guides me along right paths, bringing honor to his name. —PSALM 23:3

Even the Son of Man came not to be served but to serve others and to give his life as a ransom for many. —MARK 10:45

TODAY'S THOUGHT

Jesus sought to please his Father and give glory to him in everything he did. That plan shaped the way he lived each day and the way he served others in every interaction. As you begin each day of this year, ask yourself two questions: Will my plans for today please God? Will I be serving others today? If you can answer yes to these questions and then follow through with your actions, you will be on the right path—God's path for you. You will know how to spend your time, and you will become more like Jesus.

TODAY'S PLAN

How might asking yourself these two questions each day shape your plans?

ABILITIES

TODAY'S PROMISE

In his grace, God has given us different gifts for doing certain things well. —ROMANS 12:6

TODAY'S THOUGHT

God has empowered every person with special abilities; no one is left empty-handed. When you feel like you have nothing to offer, you can be encouraged by knowing that God has given you a unique set of abilities for a unique purpose. God promises that you do have something to offer!

TODAY'S PLAN

Have you discovered your God-given abilities?

OVERCOMING

TODAY'S PROMISE

The righteous keep moving forward, and those with clean hands become stronger and stronger. —JOB 17:9

Because the Sovereign LORD helps me, I will not be disgraced. Therefore, I have set my face like a stone, determined to do his will. And I know that I will not be put to shame. —ISAIAH 50:7

TODAY'S THOUGHT

As long as you live on this earth, you will never be free from trouble, but you can have the power to overcome it. When you allow God to work in you, he will help you overcome. When you begin to see the obstacles in your life as opportunities for God to display his power, they will not seem so overwhelming. The very hardships and weaknesses that seem to hold you back may be the tools God will use to help you overcome.

TODAY'S PLAN

Are you allowing God to turn your obstacles into his opportunities?

MATURITY

TODAY'S PROMISE

Let your roots grow down into him, and let your lives be built on him. Then your faith will grow strong in the truth you were taught, and you will overflow with thankfulness.

—COLOSSIANS 2:7

TODAY'S THOUGHT

Spiritual growth is like physical growth—you start small and grow one day at a time. As you grow, however, you need more nourishment. You get spiritual nourishment by challenging your mind in the study of God's Word, asking questions about it, and seeking answers through prayer and the counsel and experience of other believers. Look at each day as a stepping-stone, and before you know it, you will be on your way to spiritual maturity.

TODAY'S PLAN

What small step can you take today toward spiritual maturity?

APRIL

GREATNESS

TODAY'S PROMISE

Whoever wants to be first must take last place and be the servant of everyone else. —MARK 9:35

TODAY'S THOUGHT

True greatness comes from finding your real value in God's eyes. That is why humility is the essence of true greatness. Don't be fooled into striving to gain everything you desire in this world at the cost of eternal rewards in heaven. If the greatest benefactor of your achievements is yourself, then you are trying to find meaning in the wrong way.

TODAY'S PLAN

Are you living as if what you do is more important than who you are before God?

CHURCH

TODAY'S PROMISE

Just as our bodies have many parts and each part has a special function, so it is with Christ's body. We are many parts of one body, and we all belong to each other. —ROMANS 12:4-5

TODAY'S THOUGHT

God has given every believer special gifts. Some are great organizers and administrators, while others are gifted musicians, teachers, even dishwashers! When everyone in the body of Christ uses their gifts to serve each other, the church becomes a powerful force for good, a strong witness for Jesus, and a mighty army to combat Satan's attacks against the people in your community. The church needs you! The body of Christ is not complete unless you are functioning within it.

TODAY'S PLAN

What special function do you have within the church?

DISCERNMENT

TODAY'S PROMISE

People who aren't spiritual can't receive these truths from God's Spirit. It all sounds foolish to them and they can't understand it, for only those who are spiritual can understand what the Spirit means.

—1 CORINTHIANS 2:14

TODAY'S THOUGHT

Spiritual discernment involves learning to listen for the voice of the Holy Spirit, who promises to help you recognize the difference between what is true and what is false. The Holy Spirit speaks to your heart and mind, giving you a God-centered perspective on life. Those who don't have the Holy Spirit aren't spiritual, so they can't possibly have God's understanding. In fact, God's wisdom actually seems foolish to them because God's ways are so different from the world's ways. But if you have God's Spirit in you, you have God's wisdom.

TODAY'S PLAN

Are you allowing God's Holy Spirit to give you spiritual discernment?

ETERNAL LIFE

TODAY'S PROMISE

Those who die in the LORD will live; their bodies will rise again! Those who sleep in the earth will rise up and sing for joy! For your life-giving light will fall like dew on your people in the place of the dead! —ISAIAH 26:19

TODAY'S THOUGHT

Your relationship with God is eternal. It is not just for this world but will last into the world yet to come. Death is not the last chapter; it's merely a transition. As a follower of God, you have put your trust in his Son, Jesus Christ, who saves you from eternal death and gives you the gift of eternal life.

TODAY'S PLAN

Do you look at your life as eternal or temporary? How does your outlook affect the way you live today?

DELIVERANCE

TODAY'S PROMISE

*Don't be afraid. Just stand still and watch the
LORD rescue you today. . . . The LORD himself
will fight for you. Just stay calm.* —EXODUS 14:13-14

TODAY'S THOUGHT

The God who has already defeated evil is always
with you. Because you have his presence in your
life, you can be sure he will deliver you from
evil. Sometimes God will step into a situation
to rescue you. Sometimes he will send supernatural help through angels, his warriors who
are in constant battle against Satan and the powers of evil. No matter how God chooses to work,
he is always with you and promises to deliver you.

TODAY'S PLAN

*How can you make a daily habit of seeing God's hand of
deliverance working on your behalf through the events in
your life?*

FOLLOWING

TODAY'S PROMISE

All of us who have had that veil removed can see and reflect the glory of the Lord. And the Lord—who is the Spirit—makes us more and more like him as we are changed into his glorious image. —2 CORINTHIANS 3:18

TODAY'S THOUGHT

Followers pattern their lives after the person they follow. Christians are followers of Jesus Christ, and Jesus is the ultimate example of how to live in a way that is pleasing to God. While you cannot achieve perfection in this life, Jesus promises to give you the power for living effectively for him. In fact, he himself will make you more and more Christlike.

TODAY'S PLAN

What can you do today to be more like Jesus?

PRESENCE OF GOD

TODAY'S PROMISE

Be sure of this: I am with you always, even to the end of the age. —MATTHEW 28:20

TODAY'S THOUGHT

The greater your troubles, the farther away God seems. In your darkest hour, you may even feel as if God has left you. When it seems like God is absent, don't trust your feelings. Trust God's promise that he will never leave you. Rely on what the Bible tells you is true, not on what your feelings tell you.

TODAY'S PLAN

Does God seem absent to you sometimes? How can you learn to trust in his presence?

CHANGE

TODAY'S PROMISE

Heaven and earth will disappear, but my words will never disappear. —MARK 13:31

TODAY'S THOUGHT

The truths and teachings in the Bible apply to all people in all cultures in all times. The standards of living found in God's Word always apply and can always be counted on. As you face change, turn to God's unchanging Word. It will help you maintain your perspective, give your life a rock-solid foundation, and show you which way to go.

TODAY'S PLAN

When life is full of changes, do you turn to the Bible for unchanging words of comfort?

DEATH

TODAY'S PROMISE

Christ lives within you, so even though your body will die because of sin, the Spirit gives you life because you have been made right with God. —ROMANS 8:10

TODAY'S THOUGHT

When you die physically, you leave your earthly body and your place in the earthly community. But if you die spiritually, you will miss eternal life in heaven with God and with his people; you will be separated from God forever. When Christians die physically, they continue to live spiritually as they take up residence in heaven. If you believe Jesus is your Savior, death is not the end but only the beginning of an eternity of unspeakable joy in the Lord's presence with other believers.

TODAY'S PLAN

How can you learn to look at death as the beginning of true life?

ANGELS

TODAY'S PROMISE

He will order his angels to protect you wherever you go. They will hold you up with their hands so you won't even hurt your foot on a stone. —PSALM 91:11-12

TODAY'S THOUGHT

The Bible does not say whether there is one specific "guardian angel" assigned to each believer. It does say that God uses his angels to counsel, guide, protect, minister to, rescue, fight for, and care for his people. Whether he uses one specific angel or a whole host of angels to help you is his choice and your blessing. Chances are that angels have played a greater role in your life than you realize. Thank God today for the supernatural ways he cares for you.

TODAY'S PLAN

How does knowing that God sends his angels to be involved in your life affect the way you will act today?

CELEBRATION

TODAY'S PROMISE

The LORD your God . . . will take delight in you with gladness. . . . He will rejoice over you with joyful songs.

—ZEPHANIAH 3:17

TODAY'S THOUGHT

God rejoices and celebrates when his people faithfully follow him and obey his commands. If you trust God's ways and follow his commands, the very God of the universe will literally sing songs of joy because of you!

TODAY'S PLAN

What specific things can you do today that God can celebrate?

ASSUMPTIONS

TODAY'S PROMISE

*Don't make judgments about anyone ahead of time—
before the Lord returns. For he will bring our darkest
secrets to light and will reveal our private motives. Then
God will give to each one whatever praise is due.*

—1 CORINTHIANS 4:5

TODAY'S THOUGHT

False assumptions cause you to jump to conclusions and judge others. Judging others
can lead to hurtful words that threaten your
relationships. When you assume you are right,
you assume anyone who disagrees with you is
wrong. Even worse, if you set out to prove you
are right and the other person is wrong, you
might ascribe guilt to someone who is inno-
cent. God promises that if you let him be
the judge, everything will turn out fairly
in the end.

TODAY'S PLAN

*Have you ever made the wrong assumptions about
something or someone? Have you thought through
the potential consequences of jumping to the wrong
conclusions?*

RESURRECTION

TODAY'S PROMISE

Our earthly bodies are planted in the ground when we die, but they will be raised to live forever. . . . For our dying bodies must be transformed into bodies that will never die; our mortal bodies must be transformed into immortal bodies. Then, when our dying bodies have been transformed into bodies that will never die, this Scripture will be fulfilled: "Death is swallowed up in victory."

—1 CORINTHIANS 15:42, 53–54

TODAY'S THOUGHT

On the last day, every believer who has died will be resurrected. What will our new bodies be like? The Bible does say that a body fit for eternal life will be immortal, free from the limitations, disease, and death that plague our current physical existence. When aches and pains, fatigue and stress remind you that your earthly body is frail, thank Jesus for his promise of resurrection and renewal.

TODAY'S PLAN

Take a moment to imagine the perfect body you will have for your perfect life in heaven.

FEAR

TODAY'S PROMISE

Do not be afraid or discouraged, for the LORD will personally go ahead of you. He will be with you; he will neither fail you nor abandon you.

—DEUTERONOMY 31:8

TODAY'S THOUGHT

Sometimes your fears cause you to believe that God has abandoned you and left you to go it on your own. What a terrifying thought! Fear makes you feel small, alone, and hopelessly lost. But God promises that not only is he with you, he goes ahead of you and will lead you to everything he has planned for you, if you only let him.

TODAY'S PLAN

Are you afraid that God might leave you? How can you live fearlessly today because of the knowledge that he never will?

BELONGING

TODAY'S PROMISE

No one can serve two masters. For you will hate one and love the other; you will be devoted to one and despise the other. You cannot serve both God and money.

—MATTHEW 6:24

TODAY'S THOUGHT

You cannot belong to both God and the world. When you belong to the world, you will pursue worldly pleasures, which are self-indulgent. When you belong to God, you will say and do things that conflict with what the culture values. Don't let your energies become divided between two opposing sides. Decide today who you belong to.

TODAY'S PLAN

Would others say that you belong to the world or to God?

HOLY SPIRIT

TODAY'S PROMISE

Don't you realize that your body is the temple of the Holy Spirit, who lives in you and was given to you by God? You do not belong to yourself, for God bought you with a high price. So you must honor God with your body.
— 1 CORINTHIANS 6:19-20

TODAY'S THOUGHT

Part of asking the Holy Spirit to live in you and work through you involves taking care of your body, which is now the home of the Holy Spirit. Keep your body healthy with proper sleep, nutrition, and exercise so you can be more receptive to the Spirit's instructions. Keep your body pure and holy by avoiding sin and temptation so that you are available to do God's work when he calls. When you give yourself and your body to God, you receive the wonderful blessing of his Spirit working unhindered through you.

TODAY'S PLAN

Are you hindering the work of the Holy Spirit by not taking care of your body?

IMPOSSIBLE

TODAY'S PROMISE

Nothing is impossible with God. —LUKE 1:37

TODAY'S THOUGHT

There should be no doubt that God specializes in doing what from a human perspective is impossible. But the end of your abilities is the beginning of his. The God who spoke all creation into being can do the impossible for you. You must believe that he can and that he wants to.

TODAY'S PLAN

What impossible thing do you need God to do for you today?

HEAVEN

TODAY'S PROMISE

You must remain faithful to what you have been taught from the beginning. If you do, you will remain in fellowship with the Son and with the Father. And in this fellowship we enjoy the eternal life he promised us.

—1 JOHN 2:24-25

TODAY'S THOUGHT

In heaven, God will fulfill our deepest long-ings. This life, even at its best, always leaves us a bit dissatisfied. Experiences don't usually live up to expectations. Dreams go unfulfilled, and we long for so much more. These longings con-firm that our souls are anticipating something more than what this life can deliver. One day your disappointments will vanish and you will receive your heart's desires with the God who has promised the best for you and will spend an eternity delivering on that promise.

TODAY'S PLAN

Have you ever thought of unfulfilled longings as your soul anticipating the blessings of heaven?

AVOIDANCE

TODAY'S PROMISE

*Come close to God, and God will come close to you.
Wash your hands, you sinners; purify your hearts, for
your loyalty is divided between God and the world.*

—JAMES 4:8

TODAY'S THOUGHT

Avoiding some things will harm you, but avoiding other things will help you. The key is
understanding the difference. Staying away
from metal during an electrical storm can
save your life. But the strong metal frame of a
car can save your life in an accident. In matters
of faith, you should try to avoid sin at all costs
because it can be deadly. But avoiding God's
divine guidance can be just as deadly. Instead
of avoiding God, approach him. He promises that you will develop a relationship with
him and discover the difference between the
things you should and should not avoid.

TODAY'S PLAN

Have you been avoiding sin or avoiding God?

BEHAVIOR

TODAY'S PROMISE

Jesus replied, "But even more blessed are all who hear the word of God and put it into practice." —LUKE 11:28

TODAY'S THOUGHT

Faith alone is enough for salvation, but your behavior provides the evidence that your faith is genuine. If your sinful behavior doesn't change after you become a Christian, then people will wonder if your confession of faith is really genuine. Have you asked God to forgive your sins, come into your life, and transform you from the inside out? When people see godly behavior in you, they will want to know what motivates you, what makes you different. Then you will have a wonderful opportunity to tell them about your faith in God, and he will bless you for it.

TODAY'S PLAN

Can others see God when they look at your behavior?

ANGER

TODAY'S PROMISE

Morning, noon, and night I cry out in my distress, and the LORD hears my voice. —PSALM 55:17

TODAY'S THOUGHT

Any close relationship must include honesty, even if it reveals less-than-noble feelings. The truth is that you do sometimes get mad at God. Perhaps it's when you don't understand why God allows oppressors to succeed or tragedies to occur. Your anger affirms God's omnipotence because it is based on the conviction that God is in control and could have arranged circumstances differently. When you express your anger to the Lord, you express your faith that he hears you and has the power to help you.

TODAY'S PLAN

Are you angry at God? Honestly express your feelings to him, and he will listen.

DESIRES

TODAY'S PROMISE

I will give you a new heart, and I will put a new spirit in you. I will take out your stony, stubborn heart and give you a tender, responsive heart. —EZEKIEL 36:26

TODAY'S THOUGHT

When you commit your life to God, he gives you a new heart, a new nature, and a new desire to please him. When God stirs your heart, your desires will be in line with his so that what you want to do will be what he wants you to do. God's will for you becomes your greatest desire. There is nothing more wonderful than having your desires match God's!

TODAY'S PLAN

Are you taking full advantage of the new heart God has given you?

FAITH

TODAY'S PROMISE

We have been greatly encouraged in the midst of our troubles and suffering, dear brothers and sisters, because you have remained strong in your faith. It gives us new life to know that you are standing firm in the Lord.

—1 THESSALONIANS 3:7-8

TODAY'S THOUGHT

Faith is like a muscle; it gets stronger the more you exercise it. When you do what God asks you to do and see him bless you as a result of your obedience, your faith grows stronger. The next time God asks you to do something, you will have more confidence to take that leap of faith. And when others see your faith growing stronger, they will be encouraged and motivated in their faith as well.

TODAY'S PLAN

How can you exercise your faith this week?

GUIDANCE

TODAY'S PROMISE

You guide me with your counsel, leading me to a glorious destiny.
— PSALM 73:24

TODAY'S THOUGHT

God is always ready to guide you, but are you willing to follow where he leads? Are you willing to accept his plans and purposes for your life? Like a coach, God shows you how to train yourself in obedience and wisdom in order to prepare you to live more effectively now and to enter your eternal home. When you're ready to let God lead you, you won't have a problem determining where he wants you to go. He promises to guide you; you just have to follow.

TODAY'S PLAN

Are you following God's guidance?

GENEROSITY

TODAY'S PROMISE

You must each decide in your heart how much to give. And don't give reluctantly or in response to pressure. For God loves a person who gives cheerfully.

—2 CORINTHIANS 9:7

TODAY'S THOUGHT

Old Testament law made it clear that God wanted his people to tithe—to give him the first tenth of their income. This demonstrated their obedience and trust that God would provide for them. When Jesus came, he made it clear that he loves a cheerful giver with a generous heart. It is good to give out of obedience to God, but it is even better to give because you really want to. When you give out of a generous heart, you are looking for ways to help others, so more of God's work is accomplished. God promises to bless you generously when you give generously.

TODAY'S PLAN

How can you practice giving generously?

LOVE

TODAY'S PROMISE

Love never gives up, never loses faith, is always hopeful, and endures through every circumstance.

—1 CORINTHIANS 13:7

TODAY'S THOUGHT

One characteristic of authentic love is hope. God in his great love never gets tired of giving us second chances. He always thinks the best of you, always encourages you, and patiently waits for you to love him and others more. When you've forgotten or neglected him, he yearns for you to return so he can restore your relationship with him. He promises that when you truly learn to love, you will always have hope.

TODAY'S PLAN

How quickly do you give up on people? How can you develop the same kind of hopeful love that God has?

MEDITATION

TODAY'S PROMISE

I wait quietly before God, for my victory comes from him. . . . Let all that I am wait quietly before God, for my hope is in him.
—PSALM 62:1, 5

TODAY'S THOUGHT

Meditation is setting aside time to intention-ally think about God, talk to him, listen to him, read his Word, and study the writings of other Christians. If you don't spend any time con-necting with God, how can you expect to know what he wants from you? Meditation connects you with God, restoring your confidence in his promises, your passion for what he has called you to do, and your commitment to follow him. When you meditate on God's Word, you remember who he is and what he has done, giving you the assurance that he has much yet in store for you.

TODAY'S PLAN

How can you find more time to intentionally connect with God?

FUTURE

TODAY'S PROMISE

That is what the Scriptures mean when they say,
"No eye has seen, no ear has heard, and no mind has
imagined what God has prepared for those who love
him." But it was to us that God revealed these things
by his Spirit. For his Spirit searches out everything
and shows us God's deep secrets.

—1 CORINTHIANS 2:9-10

TODAY'S THOUGHT

God promises to reveal enough of the future
to give you hope. You know there is a heaven,
you know how to get there, and you know that
your future in heaven will be more wonderful
than you can imagine. Perhaps knowing more
details than that would be too much for
anyone to take in. God wants you to trust
him and demonstrate your belief that what
he promises will happen. Your trust in God
for the future will be an inspiration and an
example to others.

TODAY'S PLAN

What details about the future do you need to entrust
to God?

ENCOURAGEMENT

Each one of you will put to flight a thousand of the enemy, for the LORD your God fights for you, just as he has promised.

—JOSHUA 23:10

TODAY'S THOUGHT

You can be encouraged by the fact that God fights for you, regardless of the odds against you. The Bible gives us many examples: God used the young boy David to overcome the giant Goliath; God used Gideon's three hundred soldiers to defeat the countless thousands of Midianite soldiers; and God used the twelve disciples to establish the whole church. You don't have to be above average for God to do great things through you. Knowing that God works through you despite your limitations is a great encouragement.

TODAY'S PLAN

What great work is God doing through you? Do you need God's encouragement to accomplish it?

NEW NATURE

TODAY'S PROMISE

You have stripped off your old sinful nature and all its wicked deeds. Put on your new nature, and be renewed as you learn to know your Creator and become like him.
— COLOSSIANS 3:9-10

TODAY'S THOUGHT

You can't be truly wise or honest or good or peace-loving on your own because you were born with a sinful nature—a tendency and in fact a desire to sin and do wrong. But when you asked God to forgive your sins and come into your life, he gave you the gift of his Holy Spirit. Now the very presence of God lives in you and is helping you overcome your sinful desires. You have a new nature. You can be wise and honest and good and peace-loving—all characteristics of God—because God himself is living in you.

TODAY'S PLAN

How can you live today according to the new nature God has given you?

MAY

KINGDOM OF GOD

TODAY'S PROMISE

Since we are his children, we are his heirs. In fact, together with Christ we are heirs of God's glory.

—ROMANS 8:17

The world has now become the Kingdom of our Lord and of his Christ, and he will reign forever and ever. —REVELATION 11:15

TODAY'S THOUGHT

One of Satan's tricks is to blind you to your authority and identity as a citizen of God's eternal Kingdom. The King of the universe has adopted you as his own child. Like a crown prince, you can stand tall and firm against any threat on the Kingdom. All of God's authority, heavenly armies, strength, and power are available to you when you are under attack. Best of all, God's victory over evil has already been promised and guaranteed to all who are members of his kingdom.

TODAY'S PLAN

Are you using the authority and resources of your heavenly King?

SUCCESS

TODAY'S PROMISE

What do you benefit if you gain the whole world but lose your own soul? Is anything worth more than your soul?

—MATTHEW 16:26

TODAY'S THOUGHT

When it comes to success, you must decide whose rules you want to play by. Would you rather be a success in business but a failure as a parent, or vice versa? Would you rather be a success in the world's eyes or in God's eyes? In reality, these are not necessarily mutually exclusive. But if you were given these choices, what you would decide? Now is the time to decide what definition of success you will live by. The Bible teaches you to define success in terms of faithfulness to God. That is the standard by which you must measure everything else. God will reward your faithfulness even if you fail in the eyes of the world.

TODAY'S PLAN

What standard of success are you living by?

LEADERSHIP

TODAY'S PROMISE

Because of God's grace to me, I have laid the foundation like an expert builder. Now others are building on it. But whoever is building on this foundation must be very careful. For no one can lay any foundation other than the one we already have—Jesus Christ. —1 CORINTHIANS 3:10-11

TODAY'S THOUGHT

Many people in positions of leadership make plans to build upon their own legacy. But for the Christian leader, the greatest goal is to build upon Jesus' legacy of wisdom and integrity. Without God, everything else is temporary and ultimately meaningless. Whatever leadership position you are in, whether in your family, workplace, church, or community, work to lay a foundation based on the principles that Jesus taught and lived. Then you will leave a legacy that others can build on and that will truly last.

TODAY'S PLAN

What foundation have you built your legacy upon?

PURPOSE

TODAY'S PROMISE

I take joy in doing your will, my God, for your instructions are written on my heart. —PSALM 40:8

TODAY'S THOUGHT

God has both a general purpose and a specific purpose for you. In a general sense, you have been chosen by God to let the love of Jesus shine through you to make an impact on others. More specifically, God has given you unique spiritual gifts and wants you to use them to make a worthwhile contribution within your sphere of influence. The more you fulfill God's general purpose for you, the clearer your specific purpose will become.

TODAY'S PLAN

Do you keep a to-do list of things you need to accomplish each day, week, or month? If you were to reduce your entire life's goals to a list of only three or four items, what would they be? The top item on that list should come close to identifying the purpose of your life.

BLAME

TODAY'S PROMISE

Remember, when you are being tempted, do not say, "God is tempting me." God is never tempted to do wrong, and he never tempts anyone else. Temptation comes from our own desires, which entice us and drag us away. These desires give birth to sinful actions. And when sin is allowed to grow, it gives birth to death.   —JAMES 1:13-15

TODAY'S THOUGHT

It's always easier to blame someone or something else for our problems. When you blame God, you prevent yourself from experiencing his infinite love and care. God is not the author of temptation and sin—Satan is. While we cannot fully understand why God allows the existence of evil, we do know that God is able and willing to redeem our problems.

TODAY'S PLAN

When problems come, ask God to show you what good things he is planning to do through your difficult circumstances.

VICTORY

TODAY'S PROMISE

These trials will show that your faith is genuine. It is being tested as fire tests and purifies gold—though your faith is far more precious than mere gold. So when your faith remains strong through many trials, it will bring you much praise and glory and honor on the day when Jesus Christ is revealed to the whole world.

—1 PETER 1:7

TODAY'S THOUGHT

When you face trials, the enemy tempts you to let anger, bitterness, or discouragement defeat you. But you will win a spiritual victory if you trust God with your pain, confusion, and loneliness. The next time you face trouble or hardship, see it as an opportunity to be victorious by relying on God for strength. Take comfort in knowing that you have built up your endurance to fight and win over future temptation.

TODAY'S PLAN

Do you have a battle plan for spiritual victory over temptation?

APATHY

TODAY'S PROMISE

Watch out that you do not lose what we have worked so hard to achieve. Be diligent so that you receive your full reward.

—2 JOHN 1:8

TODAY'S THOUGHT

One of the best cures for apathy is hard work. When you work hard, you become focused and productive. The more productive you are, the more satisfied and fulfilled you become. Even better, when you see your hard work as an act of service to God, you gain more passion as you see God working through you to bless others.

TODAY'S PLAN

In what area of your life do you feel apathetic? How might hard work help you regain your passion?

WORK

TODAY'S PROMISE

*To enjoy your work and accept your lot in life—this is
indeed a gift from God.* —ECCLESIASTES 5:19

TODAY'S THOUGHT

You can be sure that work is part of God's plan
for your life and that your work matters to God.
Those who work diligently experience many
blessings and are able to pass them on to others.
At its best, work honors God and brings meaning and joy to life. In your work, you should
model characteristics of God's work, such as
excellence, concern for the well-being of others,
purpose, creativity, and service. When you have
the perspective that you are actually working for
God, your focus moves off the task itself and
allows you to enjoy your work.

TODAY'S PLAN

*How can you honor God through the work you will do
today?*

OBEDIENCE

TODAY'S PROMISE

If you look carefully into the perfect law that sets you free, and if you do what it says and don't forget what you heard, then God will bless you for doing it.

—JAMES 1:25

TODAY'S THOUGHT

God empowers you for whatever he asks you to do. You can have the energy and desire to obey him, as he commands, because he gives you his Holy Spirit to help you. Just as the air you breathe empowers your body to function, so the Holy Spirit empowers your spirit to obey. God's forgiveness frees you from bondage to sin so that, with the help of his Spirit, you are willing and able to obey him. He promises to bless your obedience.

TODAY'S PLAN

How has God empowered you to obey him?

PROMISES OF GOD

TODAY'S PROMISE

All of God's promises have been fulfilled in Christ with a resounding "Yes!" And through Christ, our "Amen" (which means "Yes") ascends to God for his glory.
— 2 CORINTHIANS 1:20

TODAY'S THOUGHT

You learn to trust people when you know they have a good track record, developed over time. Certainly, you can trust God—he has a spotless track record. Because God has always kept his promises, you can trust that he will continue to keep them. If you can't believe the promises of God, you can't really believe any of God's Word. If you can't believe God's Word, then you shouldn't believe in God at all. And if you don't believe in God at all, your long-term future has no hope, for there is nothing to look forward to beyond the grave. But you *can* believe—in God's promises, in his Word, in his character.

TODAY'S PLAN

Whether or not you believe in all of God's promises determines everything else you believe or don't believe about God.

REJECTION

TODAY'S PROMISE

Those the Father has given me will come to me, and I will never reject them. —JOHN 6:37

TODAY'S THOUGHT

God accepts everyone who comes to him in faith, even those who previously rejected him. You can approach God knowing that he will gladly welcome you and will always accept you. God will never say, "Sorry, I don't have time for you" or "Don't bother me." He always listens, always responds, always loves, always is there for you. God does not turn away but instead embraces you so you can receive all the blessings he promises you. In his open arms, you also find the ultimate example of how to accept others rather than rejecting them.

TODAY'S PLAN

Do you feel rejected by God? How can you learn to believe that God promises to accept you, no matter what?

REST

TODAY'S PROMISE

Only in returning to me and resting in me will you be saved. In quietness and confidence is your strength.

—ISAIAH 30:15

TODAY'S THOUGHT

It is crucial to pause from time to time to rest and restore yourself to a closer fellowship with God. When you spend time with him, you can tap into his strength and hear his voice more clearly. Maybe you find it difficult to stop and rest. You mistakenly believe that productivity requires constant activity. But sometimes you need to slow down in order to speed up—to stop awhile to let your body, mind, and spirit recover and to rediscover your purpose. When you take time to rest, you will be more energized and productive because you will have a clearer sense of what God wants you to do.

TODAY'S PLAN

How can you make time today to slow down and let God refresh you?

KINDNESS

TODAY'S PROMISE

If you give even a cup of cold water to one of the least of my followers, you will surely be rewarded.

—MATTHEW 10:42

TODAY'S THOUGHT

Your acts of kindness do not need to be major, award-winning events. Most often, the opportunities God sends your way for you to express kindness to others are small and may go completely unnoticed by anyone else. But God promises that he sees and rewards every act of kindness.

TODAY'S PLAN

Be on the lookout for opportunities to show kindness to someone else today.

SECURITY

TODAY'S PROMISE

Those who trust in the LORD are as secure as Mount Zion; they will not be defeated but will endure forever.

—PSALM 125:1

TODAY'S THOUGHT

From retirement investment portfolios to home-protection systems, we spend vast amounts of time and money on security. Financial security, personal security, job security, relational security, even national security are sooner or later threatened by the unpredictable nature of the fallen world we live in. The Bible teaches that you can trust God to be your source of lasting security. He is changeless, and his love endures forever.

TODAY'S PLAN

Are you as concerned about your eternal security as you are about your physical or financial security?

WORRY

TODAY'S PROMISE

Don't worry about anything; instead, pray about everything. Tell God what you need, and thank him for all he has done. Then you will experience God's peace, which exceeds anything we can understand. His peace will guard your hearts and minds as you live in Christ Jesus.   —PHILIPPIANS 4:6-7

TODAY'S THOUGHT

Worry is normal and natural. We worry about job security. We worry about unexpected expenses. We worry about family. We worry about the future. But too much worry can distract and paralyze you. It can even lead you to deny God's presence and work in your life. The Bible teaches that you can find rest from worry through prayer. When you admit you can't control the future and you entrust yourself and your loved ones to the God who does, you will have unfathomable peace.

TODAY'S PLAN

How can you develop the habit of praying when you start to worry?

TRUTH

TODAY'S PROMISE

Yes, what joy for those whose record the LORD has cleared of guilt, whose lives are lived in complete honesty!

—PSALM 32:2

TODAY'S THOUGHT

Deception, the opposite of truth, breaks the bond of trust that is so necessary in human relationships. Without trust, relationships deteriorate. Since God created us for relationship, both with others and with himself, it is easy to understand why God hates deception. God is truth; deception is lies. The good news is that because God is truth, he will never deceive you. You can count on him and believe everything he says. The more you model truth and honesty, the stronger your relationships will be.

TODAY'S PLAN

What priority do you place on telling the truth in your relationships?

GUIDANCE

TODAY'S PROMISE

The LORD says, "I will guide you along the best pathway for your life. I will advise you and watch over you."

—PSALM 32:8

TODAY'S THOUGHT

It may seem as if some things just happen, but much of what determines the direction of your life is part of God's plan for you. If everything happens by chance, either there is no God, or God is impersonal and detached from the human race. But the Bible says that God is real, compassionate, and deeply involved in his creation. You may not understand how certain events in your life fit into God's perfect plan, but you can be confident that God is watching over you and guiding you. He opens doors of opportunity, but you must walk through them. Will you follow where he leads?

TODAY'S PLAN

How can you recognize the doors of opportunity God opens for you today?

BIBLE

TODAY'S PROMISE

My child, listen to what I say, and treasure my commands. Tune your ears to wisdom, and concentrate on understanding. Cry out for insight, and ask for understanding. Search for them as you would for silver; seek them like hidden treasures. Then you will understand what it means to fear the LORD, and you will gain knowledge of God.

—PROVERBS 2:1-5

TODAY'S THOUGHT

The key to knowing God is knowing his Word. The Bible tells us exactly how we can know God, what it means to love and follow him, and how to experience eternal life with him. If you daily seek the wisdom of God's Word, meditate on his commands, and treasure his truths, you will not stray from him.

TODAY'S PLAN

How well do you know God? Your answer also indicates how well you know the Bible.

STRESS

TODAY'S PROMISE

We can rejoice, too, when we run into problems and trials, for we know that they help us develop endurance. And endurance develops strength of character, and character strengthens our confident hope of salvation.

—ROMANS 5:3-4

TODAY'S THOUGHT

Stress can cause you to focus on what is trivial and miss what is important. As pressure forces your perspective inward, you lose the big picture. Preoccupation with the issues of the moment blinds you to what's really important. The key to dealing with stress is to recognize it and not be surprised when it comes. In fact, you can look forward to how God will develop your endurance and strengthen your character because of it. While there are many healthy and positive ways to handle stress, make sure you ask for the help of God's Spirit that he promises to provide.

TODAY'S PLAN

How do you deal with stress?

BLESSINGS

TODAY'S PROMISE

May the LORD bless you and protect you. May the LORD smile on you and be gracious to you. May the LORD show you his favor and give you his peace.

—NUMBERS 6:24-26

TODAY'S THOUGHT

Success, prosperity, and material riches are not the most important blessings from God. Rather, peace, comfort, joy, fellowship with God, hope, and eternal life are the best blessings of all. God promises that all these blessings are yours when you trust and follow him. Will you gladly accept his offer?

TODAY'S PLAN

Do you recognize God's most important blessings in your life?

PRAYER

TODAY'S PROMISE

I love the LORD because he hears my voice and my prayer for mercy. Because he bends down to listen, I will pray as long as I have breath! —PSALM 116:1-2

TODAY'S THOUGHT

When someone listens to you—really listens—you develop a close bond because that person cares about you enough to hear what's on your heart. If someone is merciful to you when you don't deserve it, you feel a close bond because that person decided to love you rather than judge you. God listens—really listens—to each one of your prayers, no matter how simple it may be. He truly wants to hear what's on your mind. And God is merciful. Instead of judging you, he loves you and wants you to be vulnerable with him so he can develop a close bond with you. Never stop praying—God never stops listening!

TODAY'S PLAN

Do you feel as if God doesn't hear your prayers? Does today's promise change your mind?

ENDURANCE

TODAY'S PROMISE

God blesses those who patiently endure testing and temptation. Afterward they will receive the crown of life that God has promised to those who love him.

—JAMES 1:12

TODAY'S THOUGHT

Endurance is an essential quality of Jesus' followers. Though you have the promise of eternal life, you also live here and now in a fallen world where the powers of sin and Satan are out to destroy your faith. God promises that if you endure in your faith, not only will you survive but you will reign with Christ forever!

TODAY'S PLAN

When you feel like quitting your walk of faith, what motivates you to endure?

TEMPTATION

TODAY'S PROMISE

Wisdom will save you from the immoral woman, from the seductive words of the promiscuous woman.

—PROVERBS 2:16

TODAY'S THOUGHT

Adultery and other sexual sins are perhaps the greatest temptations for men. Sexual temptation is enormously powerful and often overwhelming. The Bible says that wisdom will save you from giving in to sexual temptation and suffering its devastating consequences. When you have God's wisdom, you have discernment—the ability to understand and predict the consequences of sin before you fall into it. When you have God's wisdom and use it, you will be able to recognize the early warning signs that you are moving in the wrong direction.

TODAY'S PLAN

Are you using God's wisdom to fight temptation?

SIN

TODAY'S PROMISE

Sin whispers to the wicked, deep within their hearts.
They have no fear of God at all. In their blind
conceit, they cannot see how wicked they really are.

—PSALM 36:1-2

TODAY'S THOUGHT

When you get in the habit of sinning, to the
point that it no longer bothers you, and when
you lose your fear of God, you won't be aware
of a terrible change taking place in your heart.
You will be overcome by pride and self-cen-
teredness, which narrows your field of spiritual
vision and eventually blinds you completely to
God's Word and his will. It is easier than you
might think to get to this point. Give yourself
a regular spiritual checkup to avoid becoming so blinded by sin that you can no longer
see your way back to God.

TODAY'S PLAN

Have you fallen into any sinful habits lately? Do you
care? Your answers reflect your spiritual condition.

REPENTANCE

TODAY'S PROMISE

Repent of your sins and turn to God, for the Kingdom of Heaven is near. —MATTHEW 3:2

TODAY'S THOUGHT

Have you ever had the experience of driving in an unfamiliar city and suddenly realizing you were going the wrong way on a one-way street? What you do next is a good picture of the biblical idea of repentance—you make a U-turn and change your direction as fast as you can. The Bible calls the wrong way sin. Repentance is admitting your sin and making a commitment to change the direction of your life with God's help. While repentance is not a popular concept these days, it is essential because it is the only way to arrive at your desired destination—heaven. Repentance makes change possible so you can experience God's fullest blessings, both now and for eternity.

TODAY'S PLAN

Have you repented of your sin and changed the direction of your life?

FELLOWSHIP

TODAY'S PROMISE

Where two or three gather together as my followers,
I am there among them. —MATTHEW 18:20

TODAY'S THOUGHT

Christians experience unique fellowship when they worship together. The Lord's promise to be in their presence transforms any gathering of believers. You draw strength from the testimony of God's faithfulness in the lives of others. You learn to comfort one another with the comfort you receive from the Lord. You experience real joy. And you give and receive love and forgiveness in practical ways. All of this is magnified because of the power of God among you.

TODAY'S PLAN

Are you regularly experiencing the joy and power of Christian fellowship?

OPPORTUNITIES

TODAY'S PROMISE

We must quickly carry out the tasks assigned us by the one who sent us. The night is coming, and then no one can work.

—JOHN 9:4

TODAY'S THOUGHT

God regularly places divine appointments right in front of you—opportunities to do good, to help someone in need, to share what you know about God. When you believe that God is presenting you with an opportunity, respond quickly and be willing to change your plans in order to take full advantage of what God has put before you. You will be motivated when you think of how God might use you because you've made yourself available to do his work.

TODAY'S PLAN

How can you be more aware today of the opportunities God puts in front of you?

REVENGE

TODAY'S PROMISE

God called you to do good, even if it means suffering, just as Christ suffered for you. He is your example, and you must follow in his steps. He never sinned, nor ever deceived anyone. He did not retaliate when he was insulted, nor threaten revenge when he suffered. He left his case in the hands of God, who always judges fairly.

—1 PETER 2:21-23

TODAY'S THOUGHT

Revenge is a reflex of anger. Someone does you wrong, even accidentally, and you want to strike back. But the Bible tells us not to take revenge. One wrong never justifies another. Getting back at someone only throws you into a downward spiral of sin and retaliation. Instead, follow Jesus' example: Refuse to take revenge on those who mistreat you. God promises that he will administer justice, and he is always fair.

TODAY'S PLAN

When God balances the account of your life, would you rather end up with mercy or revenge?

TEMPTATION

TODAY'S PROMISE

The temptations in your life are no different from what others experience. And God is faithful. He will not allow the temptation to be more than you can stand. When you are tempted, he will show you a way out so that you can endure. —1 CORINTHIANS 10:13

TODAY'S THOUGHT

Don't underestimate the power of Satan, but don't overestimate it either. He can tempt you, but he cannot force you to sin. He can dangle the bait in front of you, but he cannot make you take it. The Bible promises that no temptation will ever be too strong for you to resist. Even in times of overwhelming temptation, God provides you with a way out. In those times, the Holy Spirit gives you the power and the wisdom to find a way to escape.

TODAY'S PLAN

What temptation do you need an escape from?

LIMITATIONS

TODAY'S PROMISE

This High Priest of ours understands our weaknesses, for he faced all of the same testings we do, yet he did not sin. So let us come boldly to the throne of our gracious God. There we will receive his mercy, and we will find grace to help us when we need it most.

—HEBREWS 4:15-16

TODAY'S THOUGHT

God's work is not limited by your failures. In fact, God's work is often accomplished through your failures and weaknesses. He wants to display his limitless power through limited people. So he won't reject you when you fail. He encourages you to bring your failures and weaknesses to him so he can give you strength to be everything he intends you to be.

TODAY'S PLAN

What limitations are you struggling with today? How might God work through them?

ABILITIES

TODAY'S PROMISE

He takes no pleasure in the strength of a horse or in human might. No, the LORD's delight is in those who fear him, those who put their hope in his unfailing love.
— PSALM 147:10-11

TODAY'S THOUGHT

The number of abilities you have and how you use them are not based on how much God loves you. Long before you were born, God already loved you enough to send his Son to die for you. But God does take delight when your heart longs to do things that please him and bless others. Your desire to use your abilities is more important to God than how well you perform with them. The more you long to serve him, the more he will take your abilities and use them for greater purposes than you could accomplish on your own.

TODAY'S PLAN

Are you using your abilities to serve God?

JUNE

VISION

TODAY'S PROMISE

I tell you the truth, anyone who believes in me will do the same works I have done, and even greater works, because I am going to be with the Father. —JOHN 14:12

TODAY'S THOUGHT

You already have a vision of the future. Seeking God's vision breaks your bondage to small ideas that are not worthy of God or representative of his work in the world. God's vision expands your mind to greater possibilities. By aligning your vision with God's vision for your life, you will be inspired to head into your future with purpose and clarity.

TODAY'S PLAN

How can you align your vision with God's?

FUTURE

TODAY'S PROMISE

"I know the plans I have for you," says the LORD. "They are plans for good and not for disaster, to give you a future and a hope." —JEREMIAH 29:11

TODAY'S THOUGHT

Many people picture God as stern and vindictive, just watching and waiting for the chance to zap humans with bolts of misfortune. But today's promise shows the opposite. God loves you and wants only good things for you. He wants your future—both in this life and in heaven—to be bright and hopeful.

TODAY'S PLAN

How can you begin to see God's good plans for your future?

OBEDIENCE

TODAY'S PROMISE

If someone claims, "I know God," but doesn't obey God's commandments, that person is a liar and is not living in the truth. But those who obey God's word truly show how completely they love him. —1 JOHN 2:3-4

TODAY'S THOUGHT

Do you want to show how much you love God? He tells you how—obey him. And how do you do that? He tells you how—follow his commandments in the Bible, which is his instruction manual for living well and loving others. When you obey God, you demonstrate your belief that what he says is true. The more you obey him, the more you will begin to experience the blessings of obedience, and you will love God even more for showing you how to live a life of joy and fulfillment.

TODAY'S PLAN

How well are you obeying God?

ENCOURAGEMENT

TODAY'S PROMISE

Be joyful. Grow to maturity. Encourage each other. Live in harmony and peace. Then the God of love and peace will be with you. —2 CORINTHIANS 13:11

TODAY'S THOUGHT

God promises to be with those who encourage each other and who build others up. When you build others up, you affirm the gifts God has given them. And when they use those gifts properly, they fulfill the purpose for which they were created. You can play a role in releasing God's gifts in others by building them up. Then God will help you in every way he can.

TODAY'S PLAN

Who can you encourage today by building them up?

GOODNESS

TODAY'S PROMISE

Don't let evil conquer you, but conquer evil by doing good. —ROMANS 12:21

TODAY'S THOUGHT

Evil doesn't have to get the best of you. The Bible teaches that sin is evil because sin is rebellion against God. But when you spend as much time as you can doing good, there is no room in your life for sin or evil. God promises that good always conquers evil.

TODAY'S PLAN

How much of your day is spent doing good?

ADDICTION

TODAY'S PROMISE

The Holy Spirit produces this kind of fruit in our lives: love, joy, peace, patience, kindness, goodness, faithfulness, gentleness, and self-control.

—GALATIANS 5:22-23

TODAY'S THOUGHT

We all have our addictions, whether they are simply bad habits or serious dependencies. One thing all of us are dangerously addicted to is sin. We consistently—daily—disobey God's Word through sinful thoughts, words, or actions. The only cure is to submit to the control of God and his Holy Spirit. When you are under God's control, the Holy Spirit replaces the destructive things in your life with good things. God's transforming power is the only thing that can ultimately heal you of all addictions.

TODAY'S PLAN

What fruits of the Spirit can you cultivate to help break your sin addiction?

ADVERSITY

TODAY'S PROMISE

If God is for us, who can ever be against us? . . . No one—for God himself has given us right standing with himself. Who then will condemn us? No one—for Christ Jesus died for us and was raised to life for us, and he is sitting in the place of honor at God's right hand, pleading for us. —ROMANS 8:31, 33-34

TODAY'S THOUGHT

Adversity can be defined as "something acting against you." You may feel as if many things are acting against you: a betrayal at work, family disagreement, failures or disappointments, or periods of spiritual dryness. But you can be sure that God is always and forever on your side. He has chosen you, forgiven you, and purified you. He fights for you, pleads for you, and is stronger than any adversity you might face.

TODAY'S PLAN

How does the assurance that God is for you help you face adversity today?

GRIEF

TODAY'S PROMISE

The kind of sorrow God wants us to experience leads us away from sin and results in salvation. There's no regret for that kind of sorrow. But worldly sorrow, which lacks repentance, results in spiritual death.

—2 CORINTHIANS 7:10

TODAY'S THOUGHT

The Bible teaches that grief is an appropriate response to sin. When you grieve, you mourn for something you have lost. Sin causes you to lose so many things: your intimate relationship with God, the revelation of his plan for your life, the Holy Spirit's empowerment of your Christian service, wholeness in yourself and in your relationships with others, and an effective witness to others. What a huge loss! But grief and sorrow over sin leads you to ask God for forgiveness, to commit to changing your heart, and ultimately to experience the amazing grace of an almighty God.

TODAY'S PLAN

How much grief do you feel when you sin?

HOLINESS

TODAY'S PROMISE

Even before he made the world, God loved us and chose us in Christ to be holy and without fault in his eyes. —EPHESIANS 1:4

TODAY'S THOUGHT

God does not regard you as holy because you are sinless but because Jesus died to take your sins away. Only Jesus Christ has lived a sinless life, but anyone who seeks forgiveness for sin and acknowledges Jesus as Savior and Lord becomes holy and sincerely tries to live in obedience to God's Word. Because of Jesus, God sees that person as holy. What an amazing concept—God sent his Son to die for your sins, and now he sees only holiness when he looks at you!

TODAY'S PLAN

Have you accepted God's forgiveness so that he now sees you as holy?

COMPLACENCY

TODAY'S PROMISE

I know all the things you do, that you are neither hot nor cold. I wish that you were one or the other! But since you are like lukewarm water, neither hot nor cold, I will spit you out of my mouth! —REVELATION 3:15-16

TODAY'S THOUGHT

When you become complacent, you think too little about something that deserves greater attention. The Bible has strong words of warning about complacency, especially complacency toward God or toward sin. You can combat complacency with preparation and purpose. You must understand how close the enemy, Satan, is and how he might tempt you so you can prepare to ward off his attacks. You must also understand the purpose for which God made you, which will give you passion and intensity instead of complacency.

TODAY'S PLAN

Are you in danger of becoming complacent in any areas of your life? How might that affect your relationship with God and with others?

INVESTMENTS

TODAY'S PROMISE

*Three things will last forever—faith, hope, and love—
and the greatest of these is love.* —1 CORINTHIANS 13:13

TODAY'S THOUGHT

We all want to invest in something worthwhile,
something that will last. Unfortunately, we are
often shortsighted in our investments. We tend
to invest only in those things that will bring us
yields in this life, and we overlook the investments that make the biggest yields—the ones that
will compound for eternity. God tells us in the
Bible what is worth investing in and what will
maintain value beyond this life. Faith in Jesus,
hope in God's promises, and love for others are
three investments that will someday yield more
than you ever dreamed.

TODAY'S PLAN

*Are you making investments that will hold value
for eternity?*

MERCY

TODAY'S PROMISE

All praise to God, the Father of our Lord Jesus Christ. It is by his great mercy that we have been born again, because God raised Jesus Christ from the dead.

—1 PETER 1:3

TODAY'S THOUGHT

God's mercy is more than exemption from the punishment you deserve for your sins. It is receiving an undeserved gift—salvation, which is the greatest undeserved gift of all. Mercy is experiencing favor with almighty God when he forgives your sins and gives you the opportunity to live forever with him in a perfect world. You just believe—he does everything else. It is only because of God's mercy that we live and breathe, both now and for eternity. No wonder we should praise him!

TODAY'S PLAN

How often do you praise God for the mercy he shows you?

TRUST

TODAY'S PROMISE

Let us hold tightly without wavering to the hope we affirm, for God can be trusted to keep his promise.

—HEBREWS 10:23

TODAY'S THOUGHT

When you trust someone completely, you experience what God intended for relationships. Trust is vital. Without it, you can't let your guard down; you can't express what's really on your mind and heart. When you don't let yourself trust someone even though the person is trustworthy, you miss out on a relationship. If you don't trust God, you can't have a healthy relationship with him. But the problem is not with him, for he is the only One who is completely trustworthy. Let your guard down so you can experience the best of all relationships.

TODAY'S PLAN

What is keeping you from trusting God?

HERITAGE

TODAY'S PROMISE

Now we live with great expectation, and we have a priceless inheritance—an inheritance that is kept in heaven for you, pure and undefiled, beyond the reach of change and decay.

—1 PETER 1:3-4

TODAY'S THOUGHT

All of us have a heritage made up of the collection of character and personality traits of our ancestors. But there is another kind of heritage that everyone can be a part of. Regardless of your personal history, you can receive the spiritual heritage that comes from being in the family of God. All those who trust in Jesus Christ are God's children; to everyone who loves, obeys, and honors him, God promises to pass on his own spiritual heritage to them. And unlike your earthly heritage, this one will last for eternity.

TODAY'S PLAN

What kind of spiritual heritage are you leaving for your loved ones?

WORDS

TODAY'S PROMISE

Some people make cutting remarks, but the words of the wise bring healing. —PROVERBS 12:18

TODAY'S THOUGHT

Appropriate speech is rich in quality, scarce in quantity, and timely in delivery. How often have you blurted out something only to wish you could take it back because your words hurt someone? How often have you used off-color language and been convicted by your conscience? By choosing good words, even in response to someone else's inappropriate words, the Bible promises that you will bring healing and blessing to others.

TODAY'S PLAN

Take an inventory of your words today. How often do they bring healing, and how often do they bring hurt to others?

GUIDANCE

TODAY'S PROMISE

Your word is a lamp to guide my feet and a light for my path.
— PSALM 119:105

We can make our plans, but the LORD determines our steps.
— PROVERBS 16:9

TODAY'S THOUGHT

God's guidance is not like a searchlight that brightens a broad area; instead, it's more like a flashlight that illuminates just enough of the path ahead to show you where to take the next step. God has a definite plan for you, but he usually doesn't reveal it all at once. He wants you to learn to trust him each step of the way.

TODAY'S PLAN

In what area can you trust God's guidance today by taking one step forward?

REWARDS

TODAY'S PROMISE

We must all stand before Christ to be judged. We will each receive whatever we deserve for the good or evil we have done in this earthly body. —2 CORINTHIANS 5:10

TODAY'S THOUGHT

You can't take anything with you when you go to heaven, but there is a way to have something waiting for you when you arrive. God promises to reward those who are faithful to him and who leave behind a legacy of good deeds. Your good deeds don't determine whether you will go to heaven—only faith in Jesus does—but they do determine the treasures that will be waiting for you there. The Bible doesn't say what those treasures are, but it does say they will exceed your expectations if you've lived well here on earth.

TODAY'S PLAN

What rewards might be waiting for you in heaven?

RISK

TODAY'S PROMISE

Commit everything you do to the LORD. Trust him, and he will help you.

—PSALM 37:5

TODAY'S THOUGHT

Growth and success only occur at some risk. Taking a risk does not mean taking foolish chances—that's just stupidity. Taking a risk entails setting a goal, having a decent chance of achieving it, and pursuing it with a strong dose of confidence. Risk taking is actually necessary for you to grow in your relationship with God. When he calls you to do something out of your comfort zone, you must obey at the risk of failing and trust his promise to help you accomplish what he has asked you to do. Then you will grow by leaps and bounds.

TODAY'S PLAN

What are you willing to risk in order to grow in your relationship with God?

CAUTION

TODAY'S PROMISE

You will be blessed if you obey the commands of the LORD your God that I am giving you today. But you will be cursed if you reject the commands of the LORD your God and turn away from him.

—DEUTERONOMY 11:27-28

TODAY'S THOUGHT

Many promises in the Bible come with warning labels to guide you away from hurtful and destructive behaviors and toward a healthy, productive life. You appreciate a warning label on a bottle that tells you there is poison inside. You should likewise appreciate God's warnings so that you can avoid things that poison your soul and damage your quality of life. If you heed God's warnings to resist temptation and sin, you will avoid much pain and minimize the damage that sin can cause in your life.

TODAY'S PLAN

Think about the ways God's commands protect you. Which ones do you need to be more careful about following?

TRUTH

TODAY'S PROMISE

Now we see things imperfectly as in a cloudy mirror, but then we will see everything with perfect clarity. All that I know now is partial and incomplete, but then I will know everything completely, just as God now knows me completely. —1 CORINTHIANS 13:12

TODAY'S THOUGHT

In our quest for truth, we often find more gray areas than black and white. We often struggle to understand God, his ways, and his will for us, wondering if we are doing the right thing. The best way to approach our imperfect understanding here on earth is with a heavenly perspective. God promises that one day everything will be made clear for us. This keeps our search for truth focused on our ultimate goal of complete knowledge of God in heaven.

TODAY'S PLAN

How might a heavenly perspective clarify your search for truth?

PRIDE

TODAY'S PROMISE

*Pride goes before destruction, and haughtiness before
a fall.* —PROVERBS 16:18

TODAY'S THOUGHT

There is a positive, healthy side to pride—such
as when you are proud of your children or when
you take pride in your work. But the Bible often
speaks about the destructive side of pride because
it has the power to damage relationships,
including your relationship with God. Pride
keeps you from admitting your mistakes, blinds
you to your faults, and makes you believe you
are better than others or deserve special privi-
leges. It causes you to judge others, which leads
to jealousy, envy, and distrust. God promises
that pride will bring you down, so heed his
warning to avoid it.

TODAY'S PLAN

*Are you willing to ask someone you trust if he or she sees
any pride lurking in your life?*

LOYALTY

TODAY'S PROMISE

No one can serve two masters. For you will hate one and love the other, or be devoted to one and despise the other. You cannot serve both God and money.

—LUKE 16:13

TODAY'S THOUGHT

Loyalty means having an unwavering commitment to someone or something. If you claim complete loyalty to God, you cannot also claim loyalty to anything or anyone else. If commitment to God is your life goal, then all other decisions and desires must come under that goal. For example, submit your decisions about spending money to God first. Then God will help you control your spending, rather than your spending controlling you. Keep God as your number one priority, and you will not become a slave to other things that could control you.

TODAY'S PLAN

Is your life's goal to be loyal to God?

MINISTRY

TODAY'S PROMISE

These are the gifts Christ gave to the church: the apostles, the prophets, the evangelists, and the pastors and teachers. Their responsibility is to equip God's people to do his work and build up the church, the body of Christ. This will continue until we all come to such unity in our faith and knowledge of God's Son that we will be mature in the Lord, measuring up to the full and complete standard of Christ. —EPHESIANS 4:11-13

TODAY'S THOUGHT

It's easy to want to avoid the responsibilities of ministry, thinking it is something for the professionals—our pastors, worship leaders, etc. But God has called all believers into ministry because to minister to others simply means to love and serve them as Jesus would. The Bible promises that your faith will grow through faithful ministry.

TODAY'S PLAN

What are you doing to minister to others?

SACRIFICE

TODAY'S PROMISE

If any of you wants to be my follower, you must turn from your selfish ways, take up your cross daily, and follow me. If you try to hang on to your life, you will lose it. But if you give up your life for my sake, you will save it.

—LUKE 9:23-24

TODAY'S THOUGHT

We know that a short-term sacrifice is often necessary to produce a long-term gain. We refrain from buying the latest electronic gadget in order to save money for something more important. We sacrifice time and energy so our children can have the best chance of success later in life. We endure physical pain in order to meet a fitness goal or win an athletic competition. So it is with our faith. Following Jesus often calls for sacrifice now, but that sacrifice will produce blessings that will last eternally.

TODAY'S PLAN

Are you willing to sacrifice in order to excel in your faith?

MIRACLES

TODAY'S PROMISE

"Yes," says the LORD, "I will do mighty miracles for you, like those I did when I rescued you from slavery in Egypt."

—MICAH 7:15

TODAY'S THOUGHT

Maybe you think a miracle is always a dramatic event, like the dead being raised back to life. But miracles are happening all around you. These supernatural occurrences may not be as dramatic as the parting of the Red Sea, but they are no less powerful. Think of the birth of a baby, the healing of an illness, the rebirth of the earth in spring, the restoration of broken relationships through the work of love and forgiveness, the salvation of sinners through faith alone, the specific call of God in your life. And these are just a few "everyday" miracles. If you think you've never seen a miracle, look closer. They are happening all around you.

TODAY'S PLAN

How can you be more open to seeing the miracles in your life?

INJUSTICE

TODAY'S PROMISE

The righteous LORD loves justice. The virtuous will see his face.
　　　　　　　　　　　　　　　　　　　—PSALM 11:7

TODAY'S THOUGHT

You cannot ignore it when others are being treated unjustly. Otherwise you are in danger of becoming callous toward the needs of others, or even becoming corrupt. Be an advocate for justice, and your heart will move you to be a champion of those who need your help to receive fair treatment. God promises that those who work for justice will experience his presence in powerful ways.

TODAY'S PLAN

Are you moved when you see injustice around you?

OPPOSITION

TODAY'S PROMISE

God blesses those who are persecuted for doing right, for the Kingdom of Heaven is theirs. God blesses you when people mock you and persecute you and lie about you and say all sorts of evil things against you because you are my followers. Be happy about it! Be very glad! For a great reward awaits you in heaven.

—MATTHEW 5:10-12

TODAY'S THOUGHT

Your allegiance to God brings you into direct conflict with anyone opposed to God or what he stands for. This includes other people as well as supernatural powers of evil. When you choose to follow God, you must anticipate opposition from those fighting against him. But God promises that those who endure will experience blessings and joy, both in this life and in heaven.

TODAY'S PLAN

Are you experiencing any opposition because you follow God?

TESTING

TODAY'S PROMISE

The LORD your God is testing you to see if you truly love him with all your heart and soul.

—DEUTERONOMY 13:3

TODAY'S THOUGHT

The result of testing is a more committed faith. Just as commercial products are tested again and again to improve their performance, so your faith is tested to make it better and stronger so you can accomplish everything God wants you to.

TODAY'S PLAN

Are you passing the testing of your faith?

WISDOM

TODAY'S PROMISE

Give me an understanding heart so that I can . . . know the difference between right and wrong. —1 KINGS 3:9

TODAY'S THOUGHT

Solomon prayed for wisdom, and God was happy to give it to him. Asking God for wisdom pleases him because it shows that you want to live according to his ways. Life experience does not automatically produce wisdom. When life experience is filtered through a teachable spirit and prayerfully linked to the truths of Scripture, then you will have God's wisdom. God grants his wisdom to those who ask for it and value it.

TODAY'S PLAN

If you could ask God for anything, would you think to ask for wisdom?

GRIEF

TODAY'S PROMISE

The Holy Spirit helps us in our weakness. For example, we don't know what God wants us to pray for. But the Holy Spirit prays for us with groanings that cannot be expressed in words. And the Father who knows all hearts knows what the Spirit is saying, for the Spirit pleads for us believers in harmony with God's own will. —ROMANS 8:26-27

TODAY'S THOUGHT

When you are in such grief and confusion that you don't even know how to express it to God, the Holy Spirit prays for you and expresses your feelings for you. When you can't even form the words of a prayer, let the Holy Spirit intercede for you. He will pray for you when you can't even pray for yourself. He will implore God to give you the comfort you so desperately need.

TODAY'S PLAN

How does it comfort you to know that the Holy Spirit is praying for you?

JULY

RESPONSIBILITY

TODAY'S PROMISE

Don't excuse yourself by saying, "Look, we didn't know." For God understands all hearts, and he sees you. He who guards your soul knows you knew. He will repay all people as their actions deserve.

—PROVERBS 24:12

TODAY'S THOUGHT

Few people take responsibility for their own actions; they prefer to blame someone or something else. God says that you are responsible for your own conduct. If you are acting responsibly, you can be depended on to be where you are supposed to be, when you are supposed to be there, to be consistent in words and actions. Take responsibility for everything you do, and it will enhance your reputation before God and others.

TODAY'S PLAN

In what situations are you most tempted to blame others or claim ignorance? How can you learn to take responsibility when you need to?

RIGHTEOUSNESS

TODAY'S PROMISE

God made Christ, who never sinned, to be the offering for our sin, so that we could be made right with God through Christ. —2 CORINTHIANS 5:21

TODAY'S THOUGHT

Righteousness is the opposite of sin. Sin is rebellion against God, and it breaks your relationship with him. Faith is your lifeline to God. When you accept Jesus as your Savior and ask him to forgive your sins, this simple act of faith makes you righteous in God's sight. God looks at you as though you have never sinned. You can live freely without guilt, and you can be confident of eternal life.

TODAY'S PLAN

How does the knowledge that God has called you righteous affect the way you live?

GRACE

TODAY'S PROMISE

Sin is no longer your master, for you no longer live under the requirements of the law. Instead, you live under the freedom of God's grace. —ROMANS 6:14

TODAY'S THOUGHT

God's ultimate act of grace—sending his Son, Jesus, to die on the cross to save us—is the example of how you are to extend grace to others. Be quick to forgive, swift to extend kindness, generous in love—even when others don't deserve it. One of the most priceless gifts anyone can receive is the gift of grace. Grace is always undeserved and unexpected, yet so appreciated. When you extend grace to someone, you give them the same wonderful gift God has given to you so many times.

TODAY'S PLAN

Can you give someone the gift of grace today?

NATION

TODAY'S PROMISE

I urge you, first of all, to pray for all people. Ask God to help them; intercede on their behalf, and give thanks for them. Pray this way for kings and all who are in authority so that we can live peaceful and quiet lives marked by godliness and dignity. —1 TIMOTHY 2:1-2

TODAY'S THOUGHT

It's important for Christians to pray for our nation because the Bible says it leads to peace. Pray for this nation to be protected by God's mighty hand. Pray for its leaders to be humble and wise, to discern right from wrong, and to champion the cause of the needy and helpless. A nation that allows or endorses immorality is subject to judgment and will eventually collapse from the inside out. A nation that collectively worships the one true God will stand firm and live in peace.

TODAY'S PLAN

How can you pray for your country today?

JUSTICE

TODAY'S PROMISE

This is what the LORD says: "Be just and fair to all. Do what is right and good, for I am coming soon to rescue you and to display my righteousness among you."

—ISAIAH 56:1

TODAY'S THOUGHT

When you are experiencing difficult times, it is tempting to think God is not fair or just. How can he allow a Christian to suffer when so many unbelievers are prospering? The Bible tells us that justice and fairness will often be perverted in this life by selfish people. But God promises that justice will not be twisted forever. True justice will one day prevail in eternity for those who live for God. So keep fighting for justice now and rest in the fact that God will set everything right in the future.

TODAY'S PLAN

How can you focus less on your own injustices and more on bringing justice to those who are oppressed?

ENCOURAGEMENT

TODAY'S PROMISE

As soon as I pray, you answer me; you encourage me by giving me strength. —PSALM 138:3

TODAY'S THOUGHT

Prayer allows your heart to receive God's encouragement. When you talk to God in prayer, he reassures you of his presence and his plans for good in your life. Through prayer, God gives you the strength you need to be encouraged, refreshed, and prepared for what lies ahead.

TODAY'S PLAN

Are you discouraged? Have you opened your heart to receiving God's encouragement through prayer?

SUFFERING

TODAY'S PROMISE

He has not ignored or belittled the suffering of the needy. He has not turned his back on them, but has listened to their cries for help.

—PSALM 22:24

TODAY'S THOUGHT

God does not promise believers a life free from pain and suffering. If Christians didn't hurt, other people might only see God as some sort of magician who takes away all the bad things in life. But because you have a relationship with God, he helps you, comforts you, and sometimes miraculously heals your pain. Most importantly, God will one day take away all of your suffering when you arrive in heaven. Whatever pain you are experiencing is only temporary. Perhaps it will end here on earth, but you can be certain there is no suffering in heaven.

TODAY'S PLAN

Are you longing for an end to your suffering? Try to picture the eternity free from pain that God promises you.

CRISIS

TODAY'S PROMISE

God is our refuge and strength, always ready to help in times of trouble. So we will not fear when earthquakes come and the mountains crumble into the sea.

—PSALM 46:1-2

TODAY'S THOUGHT

You need not pray for the Lord to be with you in times of crisis—he already is. Pray that you will be aware of his presence and that you will have the presence of mind to ask for his help. He promises to help you and strengthen you, so don't be afraid when crisis hits.

TODAY'S PLAN

When you face a crisis, do you turn to God for help?

TROUBLE

TODAY'S PROMISE

Don't let your hearts be troubled. Trust in God, and trust also in me. . . . I am leaving you with a gift—peace of mind and heart. And the peace I give is a gift the world cannot give. So don't be troubled or afraid.

—JOHN 14:1, 27

TODAY'S THOUGHT

Trouble creates stress. Stress, in turn, creates more trouble. The Bible indicates that trouble enters your life from a variety of sources— including your own behavior and decisions. But it is comforting to know that God promises to make his comfort, peace, and rest available to you. Will you accept them and make use of them?

TODAY'S PLAN

Do you have God's peace despite the trouble in your life?

TEAMWORK

TODAY'S PROMISE

Two people are better off than one, for they can help each other succeed. If one person falls, the other can reach out and help. But someone who falls alone is in real trouble. . . . Three are even better, for a triple-braided cord is not easily broken.

—ECCLESIASTES 4:9-12

TODAY'S THOUGHT

Accomplishments can be multiplied through teamwork. It is impossible for one person to create the harmony of a duet or a trio. You can't play a team sport like football or soccer without teamwork. It is hard to have a happy marriage if only one partner works at it. That's why God encourages us in the Bible that two people working together can do much more than one, as long as they are pulling in the same direction.

TODAY'S PLAN

Do you prefer to go it alone? How might you benefit from cooperation and teamwork?

SATISFACTION

TODAY'S PROMISE

He satisfies the thirsty and fills the hungry with good things.
—PSALM 107:9

Jesus replied, "I am the bread of life. Whoever comes to me will never be hungry again. Whoever believes in me will never be thirsty."
—JOHN 6:35

TODAY'S THOUGHT

Getting more and more of something does not necessarily bring satisfaction. In fact, it isn't long before we want even more. Only God can fulfill our deepest longings. He designed us to find satisfaction in him alone. When you discover that only a relationship with him truly satisfies, you will stop longing for things that can never satisfy.

TODAY'S PLAN

How are you trying to satisfy your deepest longings?

INTEGRITY

TODAY'S PROMISE

People with integrity walk safely, but those who follow crooked paths will slip and fall.   —PROVERBS 10:9

TODAY'S THOUGHT

Integrity involves having a stable character. If you are known as a person who always keeps his word and tries to do what is right, then your life has integrity. Others will trust you because they know they can count on you. You are as good as your word. God promises that when you have integrity, you will walk safely through life.

TODAY'S PLAN

What can you do today to develop a life of integrity?

ANGER

TODAY'S PROMISE

Sensible people control their temper; they earn respect by overlooking wrongs.

—PROVERBS 19:11

TODAY'S THOUGHT

Learning to bring your emotions under the control of the Holy Spirit is part of the process of spiritual maturity. Anger can either be a legitimate emotional response or a volatile reaction that hurts others and destroys relationships. It must be dealt with quickly before it turns into bitterness, hatred, or revenge. When anger begins to well up inside you, stop and ask yourself, *Who is really offended in this situation? Is this about God's honor or my pride? Am I acting out of humility or revenge?* Confession, forgiveness, and reconciliation will melt your anger away.

TODAY'S PLAN

In what kinds of situations do you need to control your anger?

STRENGTH

TODAY'S PROMISE

It is not by force nor by strength, but by my Spirit, says the LORD of Heaven's Armies. —ZECHARIAH 4:6

TODAY'S THOUGHT

Sometimes you need to keep working, even though you feel exhausted. When you are tired and need to finish a task, pray to God for strength to keep going until you reach a stopping point or until the work is completed. There is a spiritual strength that only God can give you, and you can receive it simply by asking. The end of your strength is the beginning of his.

TODAY'S PLAN

Do you need God's strength today to help you keep going?

OBEDIENCE

TODAY'S PROMISE

Obey me, and I will be your God, and you will be my people. Do everything as I say, and all will be well!

—JEREMIAH 7:23

TODAY'S THOUGHT

Obedience can be defined as being submissive to an authority. Ironically, obedience to God and his commands actually frees you to enjoy life as he intended it to be. Obedience keeps you from becoming entangled in or enslaved to sin that distracts or hurts you. It protects you from evil and leads you on godly paths. God promises that when you obey him, you will find blessing and opportunities for service that will please him.

TODAY'S PLAN

Can you learn to see obedience to God as freeing rather than restricting?

PRODUCTIVITY

TODAY'S PROMISE

A good tree can't produce bad fruit, and a bad tree can't produce good fruit. A tree is identified by its fruit. . . . A good person produces good things from the treasury of a good heart, and an evil person produces evil things from the treasury of an evil heart. What you say flows from what is in your heart.

—LUKE 6:43-45

TODAY'S THOUGHT

An apple might look good on the outside but actually be full of worms. In the same way, the fruit God desires in you is not the external appearance of goodness but the internal reality of a heart that truly wants to love and serve him. Pretending to be spiritual will eventually reveal a rotten core that cannot be productive. A genuinely good heart will produce good things.

TODAY'S PLAN

How does the condition of your heart on the inside affect what others see on the outside?

REST

TODAY'S PROMISE

The LORD is my shepherd; I have all that I need.
He lets me rest in green meadows; he leads me beside
peaceful streams. He renews my strength. He guides
me along right paths, bringing honor to his name.

—PSALM 23:1-3

TODAY'S THOUGHT

Rest isn't just for leisure or for vacation. Rest
plays an essential role in your ability to keep
going. It renews your energy, restores your
strength, and reignites your passion. We often
take pride in telling others how busy we are, and
we feel vaguely guilty when we relax. But God did
not intend for his people to live in a state of
frenzied activity. God teaches us in his Word
that we need the renewal of our body and
spirit that comes from rest.

TODAY'S PLAN

Are you getting enough rest to renew your body and spirit?

QUITTING

TODAY'S PROMISE

Let's not get tired of doing what is good. At just the right time we will reap a harvest of blessing if we don't give up.

—GALATIANS 6:9

TODAY'S THOUGHT

When you can see the finish line ahead of you, it's easier to keep going instead of quitting; somehow you can find enough energy to make it to the end. The race of life is no different. Sometimes it seems too long and too hard, and all you want to do is give up. But there is a finish line ahead—heaven. Everyone who crosses the finish line wins and receives rewards beyond imagination. So keep your eyes on heaven, and don't give up when life gets tough.

TODAY'S PLAN

How can you find the energy to keep going when you feel like quitting?

WITNESSING

TODAY'S PROMISE

You will receive power when the Holy Spirit comes upon you. And you will be my witnesses, telling people about me everywhere—in Jerusalem, throughout Judea, in Samaria, and to the ends of the earth. —ACTS 1:8

TODAY'S THOUGHT

Don't just assume that someone won't respond to the Good News about Jesus. In God's hands, the worst sinner can become the mightiest Christian leader. God promises that he will empower anyone who wants to share his message with others. The power of the Holy Spirit is all you need to be an effective witness for Christ.

TODAY'S PLAN

Do you know someone who you think would never respond to God's good news of salvation? Perhaps God wants you to witness to that person.

ASSURANCE

TODAY'S PROMISE

I prayed to the LORD, and he answered me. He freed me from all my fears. —PSALM 34:4

TODAY'S THOUGHT

Prayer deepens your assurance of God's love for you and his ability to carry out his promises. Sometimes we fear that God doesn't hear us or isn't actually involved in our lives. But your conversations with God remind you that he is truly there, he is involved, and he answers you. As you feel a sense of peace from spending time in prayer with God, you will have the assurance that he is listening to you and will always keep his promises to you.

TODAY'S PLAN

Do you have the assurance that God hears your prayers and answers them?

BUSYNESS

TODAY'S PROMISE

Teach us to realize the brevity of life, so that we may grow in wisdom.
—PSALM 90:12

Make the most of every opportunity in these evil days. Don't act thoughtlessly, but understand what the Lord wants you to do.
—EPHESIANS 5:16–17

TODAY'S THOUGHT

It's ironic, but a busy week can become seven days of empty activities. The key to avoiding meaningless busyness is to be fully productive for God. Busyness can be your biggest enemy if it keeps you from pausing to evaluate what is really important, including the people God has put in your life and the purpose for which he has called you. When you realize how short life is, you will gain wisdom and be able to order your life according to God's priorities instead of the world's.

TODAY'S PLAN

Are you busy doing what God wants you to do, or are you just plain busy?

GREATNESS

TODAY'S PROMISE

No one can measure his greatness. —PSALM 145:3

[The LORD] is the Potter, and he is certainly greater than you, the clay! —ISAIAH 29:16

TODAY'S THOUGHT

Because of our limited human perspective, we sometimes assign worth to created things rather than to the Creator of all things. In reality, created things are meant to point to God. When you learn to see the glory of God in his creation, you realize that his greatness is beyond human understanding and that he alone is worthy of praise and worship.

TODAY'S PLAN

Make a deliberate effort today to notice something in God's creation that points to the greatness of God.

CALL OF GOD

TODAY'S PROMISE

*I knew you before I formed you in your mother's womb.
Before you were born I set you apart and appointed
you as my prophet to the nations.* —JEREMIAH 1:5

TODAY'S THOUGHT

You might think that God was only speaking to
the prophet Jeremiah in these verses. But God
calls everyone to do a certain job, to accomplish
a specific task, or to use their gifts in a unique
way. When God calls you to do something, he
will make sure you know what it is. Often you
will feel a strong sense of leading from him. It's
up to you to respond and walk through the door
of opportunity he opens.

TODAY'S PLAN

*Do you have a strong sense that God is leading you in a
certain direction or asking you to serve him in some way?
How can you begin to respond to God's call in practical
ways today?*

CELEBRATION

TODAY'S PROMISE

You have turned my mourning into joyful dancing. You have taken away my clothes of mourning and clothed me with joy, that I might sing praises to you and not be silent. O LORD my God, I will give you thanks forever!

—PSALM 30:11-12

TODAY'S THOUGHT

Those who have faced the greatest hardships are often the ones who most appreciate and celebrate the good times when they come. And times of celebration will come—if not in this life, certainly in heaven. God promises that the bitter seeds of tears, grief, and mourning will yield a harvest of joy, blessing, and celebration.

TODAY'S PLAN

Can you try to imagine the heavenly celebrations that God promises you will one day participate in?

HEAVEN

TODAY'S PROMISE

I saw a new heaven and a new earth. . . . And I saw the holy city, the new Jerusalem, coming down from God out of heaven like a bride beautifully dressed for her husband. I heard a loud shout from the throne, saying, "Look, God's home is now among his people! He will live with them, and they will be his people."

—REVELATION 21:1-3

TODAY'S THOUGHT

Many places on earth are special to us because they give us glimpses of our eternal home in heaven. The glory of the old Jerusalem gave God's people a glimpse of the even more glorious new Jerusalem. The beauty of creation, genuine love between friends and family, times and places of rest and renewal—all of these are just a taste of the perfect beauty, love, rest, and renewal of heaven. Then we will experience everything the way God originally intended it to be.

TODAY'S PLAN

Do you long for your eternal home in heaven? What things or people in your life give you a glimpse of heaven?

CELEBRATION

TODAY'S PROMISE

Sing for joy, O heavens! Rejoice, O earth! Burst into song, O mountains! For the LORD has comforted his people and will have compassion on them in their suffering.
                                        —ISAIAH 49:13

TODAY'S THOUGHT

God gives us the ultimate reason to celebrate because he has rescued us from the consequences of sin, he comforts us now, and he promises us the wonders of eternity. Celebration can be a powerful way to renew your hope because it takes the focus off your current troubles and puts it on God's blessings and on God himself. God's people truly have the most to celebrate!

TODAY'S PLAN

What blessings from God can you celebrate with friends or family this week?

VICTORY

TODAY'S PROMISE

Thank God! He gives us victory over sin and death through our Lord Jesus Christ. —1 CORINTHIANS 15:57

TODAY'S THOUGHT

There is no greater victory—in this life or the next—than winning eternal life through faith in Jesus. Living forever in heaven is the best reward anyone could receive. You will be able to handle any defeat with grace because Jesus has already achieved the ultimate victory for you.

TODAY'S PLAN

Have you considered the fact that because of Jesus, you've already won life's greatest victory?

PRAYER

TODAY'S PROMISE

Keep on asking, and you will receive what you ask for. Keep on seeking, and you will find. Keep on knocking, and the door will be opened to you. For everyone who asks, receives. Everyone who seeks, finds. And to everyone who knocks, the door will be opened.
—MATTHEW 7:7-8

TODAY'S THOUGHT

There's more to prayer than just getting an answer to a question or a solution to a problem. God often does more in your heart through your act of praying than he does in actually answering your prayer. As you persist in talking and listening to God, he promises you will gain greater understanding of yourself, your situation, your motivation, and God's purpose and direction for you and your life.

TODAY'S PLAN

How can your prayer life be a conversation with God?

FUTURE

TODAY'S PROMISE

Because we are united with Christ, we have received an inheritance from God, for he chose us in advance, and he makes everything work out according to his plan.

—EPHESIANS 1:11

TODAY'S THOUGHT

When you take Jesus Christ as your Lord, you are guaranteed eternal life in heaven. The promise of this future inheritance changes the way you live. You can discover and take part in the plan God has for you. You can be confident that nothing can harm your soul or your eternal future. You can take risks and walk in faith when you think God is asking you to do something for him. You can be generous and experience peace of mind. You can live as if your future is everything you could ask for—because it is.

TODAY'S PLAN

How will God's promise that your eternal future is secure change the way you live today?

WORSHIP

TODAY'S PROMISE

Oh, how great are God's riches and wisdom and knowledge! How impossible it is for us to understand his decisions and his ways! For who can know the LORD's thoughts? Who knows enough to give him advice? And who has given him so much that he needs to pay it back? For everything comes from him and exists by his power and is intended for his glory.

—ROMANS 11:33-36

TODAY'S THOUGHT

Take a moment to praise God whenever you see his wisdom, power, guidance, care, and love in your life. Then worship will become a way of life.

TODAY'S PLAN

Take a moment to worship God right now.

VISION

TODAY'S PROMISE

The people's minds were hardened, and to this day whenever the old covenant is being read, the same veil covers their minds so they cannot understand the truth. And this veil can be removed only by believing in Christ. —2 CORINTHIANS 3:14

TODAY'S THOUGHT

For many of us, the only way we can see clearly is by covering our eyes with corrective lenses! With spiritual vision, you need to see through the lens of faith. You need to believe that there is much more happening around you than what you can actually see. When you find yourself unable to understand what God wants you to do, remember that your faith in Christ opens your spiritual eyes to see God's vision for you.

TODAY'S PLAN

How can you develop better spiritual vision?

AUGUST

COMMITMENT

TODAY'S PROMISE

Seek the LORD while you can find him. Call on him now while he is near. Let the wicked change their ways and banish the very thought of doing wrong. Let them turn to the LORD that he may have mercy on them.

—ISAIAH 55:6-7

TODAY'S THOUGHT

God wants a commitment of your whole self, your whole life. Four steps are involved in a wholehearted commitment to the Lord: You must (1) seek a relationship with God; (2) call on God for help and salvation; (3) turn from your sinful habits; and (4) commit yourself to living in faith and obedience to God. When you commit to doing these things, God commits to sending his Holy Spirit to live in you.

TODAY'S PLAN

Have you already taken these four steps toward commitment? Ask God to help you commit your whole life to him.

POSSESSIONS

TODAY'S PROMISE

Those who love money will never have enough. How meaningless to think that wealth brings true happiness!

—ECCLESIASTES 5:10

TODAY'S THOUGHT

The pursuit of money and possessions can easily deceive you into thinking, *If only I had a little more, then I would be content.* The Bible promises that nothing could be further from the truth. Contentment is based not on how much material wealth you have but on how much spiritual wealth you have. The love of material things can become a deadly trap. You can avoid this trap if you are willing to give up your material possessions so you can store up spiritual treasures in heaven. God may not ask you to, but if you are at least willing, you will have a healthy attitude toward possessions.

TODAY'S PLAN

Are you content with the possessions you have, or are you always wanting more?

EMPTINESS

TODAY'S PROMISE

Like newborn babies, you must crave pure spiritual milk so that you will grow into a full experience of salvation. Cry out for this nourishment. —1 PETER 2:2

TODAY'S THOUGHT

When our hearts are empty, we try to fill them with anything—even if it's evil and destructive. That's the kind of opportunity Satan looks for. He is always ready to move into an empty heart, to deceive you into thinking that what he offers can satisfy your emptiness. To keep sin and Satan out, you must keep your heart nourished with the love, truth, and goodness of God's Word and the presence of the Holy Spirit. Then there won't be any room for evil to enter.

TODAY'S PLAN

How do you try to fill the emptiness in your soul? Can you learn to crave spiritual nourishment?

PAIN

TODAY'S PROMISE

He will wipe every tear from their eyes, and there will be no more death or sorrow or crying or pain. All these things are gone forever. —REVELATION 21:4

TODAY'S THOUGHT

Whether it is from betrayal, neglect, or abandonment, physical injury or failing health—the result is some kind of emotional or physical pain. We've all experienced the debilitating feeling of an ill or wounded body or the ache of a broken heart. Your greatest hope in times of pain is to find healing in God. Although he does not promise to remove your pain in this life, he does promise to be with you in it and give you hope and purpose, despite your hurting body and soul. Most importantly, God promises to remove your pain forever in heaven.

TODAY'S PLAN

Where do you hurt the most—in your body or heart? Do you trust God's promise to take all your pain away someday?

POTENTIAL

TODAY'S PROMISE

Now all glory to God, who is able, through his mighty power at work within us, to accomplish infinitely more than we might ask or think.
—EPHESIANS 3:20

TODAY'S THOUGHT

God brings out the best in you, and he sees more in you than you see in yourself. You look at your limitations, but God looks at your potential. If you want a new perspective, learn to see life through God's eyes. He doesn't put nearly as many limitations on you as you put on yourself. He sees you for what he intended you to be as well as for what you are—forgiven and empowered through faith in Jesus, his Son.

TODAY'S PLAN

What would you like God to accomplish through you? Do you believe he can do it?

SPIRITUAL WARFARE

TODAY'S PROMISE

Stay alert! Watch out for your great enemy, the devil. He prowls around like a roaring lion, looking for someone to devour. Stand firm against him, and be strong in your faith. —1 PETER 5:8-9

TODAY'S THOUGHT

Sin is like war—it always destroys, sometimes dramatically, sometimes slowly. Sin invades your life, threatening to take over and claim territory in your heart. When sin is given free reign in your heart or temptation is allowed to lurk around the edges of your life, it is like an invading enemy army that seeks to conquer and enslave you. But when you fight against sin and remove it piece by piece from your life, God promises that you will experience the victorious Christian life and all the blessings that come along with it.

TODAY'S PLAN

What is your battle plan against the sin in your life?

CONFESSION

TODAY'S PROMISE

Everyone who believes in him will have their sins forgiven through his name.

— ACTS 10:43

TODAY'S THOUGHT

When you confess your sins, you agree with God that something wrong needs to be made right and that your damaged relationship needs to be restored. Confession is the act of recognizing your sins before God so he can forgive you. Sin separates you from a holy God; confession indicates your desire to be in a right relationship with him. God promises that everyone who confesses their sins and believes in him will be forgiven.

TODAY'S PLAN

Is sin damaging your relationship with God? Confess and receive God's forgiveness.

PAST

TODAY'S PROMISE

O LORD my God, you have performed many wonders for us. Your plans for us are too numerous to list. You have no equal. If I tried to recite all your wonderful deeds, I would never come to the end of them.

—PSALM 40:5

Who can list the glorious miracles of the LORD? Who can ever praise him enough? —PSALM 106:2

TODAY'S THOUGHT

The past helps you remember what God has done for you. Remembering how God has worked in the past—both for you and for God's people—gives you confidence and hope that he will continue his great work in the future. Every miracle and wonderful work of the Lord—past and present—is an assurance for the future.

TODAY'S PLAN

How has God blessed you in the past? How does this give you confidence that he will work in your future?

OVERWHELMED

TODAY'S PROMISE

O LORD, I have so many enemies; so many are against me. . . . But you, O LORD, are a shield around me; you are my glory, the one who holds my head high. . . . Victory comes from you, O LORD.

—PSALM 3:1, 3, 8

TODAY'S THOUGHT

The powers of evil can seem overwhelming at times. You may wonder how you can keep going. But God says not to be afraid because he will act like a shield around you. When you are afraid, the courage you need comes only from realizing how powerful God is. Then the odds won't seem so impossible. No enemy can stand before him. God is more powerful than any force against you.

TODAY'S PLAN

Are you feeling overwhelmed? How can you learn to trust God for victory?

ACCOUNTABILITY

TODAY'S PROMISE

We don't live for ourselves or die for ourselves. If we live, it's to honor the Lord. And if we die, it's to honor the Lord. So whether we live or die, we belong to the Lord. . . . Yes, each of us will give a personal account to God. —ROMANS 14:7-8, 12

TODAY'S THOUGHT

The purpose of life is to honor God. Is anyone helping you do that? How do you know if you're doing it well? You need someone to keep you accountable. Don't wait until the end of your life to find out from God if you lived it well—or didn't. Go to him now by reading his Word, and make sure that your thoughts, words, and actions are in tune with his and honor him. Ask godly friends how you are honoring God. Accountability keeps you honest and on the right path so that when you come face-to-face with God, you can be sure he will be pleased.

TODAY'S PLAN

Are you making use of God's Word, prayer, and godly friends to keep you accountable?

HEAVEN

TODAY'S PROMISE

There is more than enough room in my Father's home. If this were not so, would I have told you that I am going to prepare a place for you?

—JOHN 14:2

TODAY'S THOUGHT

When you travel, you often make reservations at a hotel because it's comforting to know you have a place to stay at the end of the day. You can have this same comfort for the end of your life's journey. Though death is a great unknown, Jesus Christ has gone before you, and he is preparing a glorious place for you to stay. If you know and love Jesus, you can be confident that your room is ready and waiting.

TODAY'S PLAN

Are you confident that Jesus is preparing a place for you in heaven?

OPPORTUNITIES

TODAY'S PROMISE

Keep watch and pray, so that you will not give in to temptation. For the spirit is willing, but the body is weak!
—MATTHEW 26:41

TODAY'S THOUGHT

Pray that God will prepare you to notice and respond to opportunities when they come to you. Prayer is a good way to stay alert and on the lookout for how God wants to work in your life. Prayer keeps you connected to God and spiritually sensitive so you can recognize his voice and his call to discern if an opportunity is from him and if he wants you to act on it. Left to ourselves, we miss much. But when God connects with your spirit, you will hear and see so much more.

TODAY'S PLAN

Are you staying connected to God so you can take the opportunities he sends you?

FAITH

TODAY'S PROMISE

Faith is the confidence that what we hope for will actually happen; it gives us assurance about things we cannot see.

— HEBREWS 11:1

TODAY'S THOUGHT

Faith is confident assurance that what you believe is really going to happen. Faith gives you hope. When the world seems like a crazy, mixed-up place, believers can be absolutely confident that one day Jesus will come back and make everything right again. Your faith in his promises will help you keep going today.

TODAY'S PLAN

How does your faith in God's future give you hope for today?

CULTURE

TODAY'S PROMISE

The world would love you as one of its own if you belonged to it, but you are no longer part of the world. I chose you to come out of the world, so it hates you.

—JOHN 15:19

TODAY'S THOUGHT

Jesus explains that if you are truly following him rather than the world, you will be misunderstood, possibly even mocked and persecuted. God's message is countercultural. When you follow his ways—for example, pray for your enemies or give your money to help others—it will not make sense according to today's cultural standards. As a result, you can expect some ridicule and opposition. But that won't always be the norm. In God's new culture in heaven, goodness and righteousness will be the norm. So think of yourself as ahead of your time!

TODAY'S PLAN

Is the way you live each day countercultural?

INTENTIONS

TODAY'S PROMISE

It is better to say nothing than to make a promise and not keep it.

—ECCLESIASTES 5:5

TODAY'S THOUGHT

There are no rewards for good intentions. If you intend to become a Christian "someday" but never get around to it, you forfeit the reward of heaven. If you intend to hug your kids each day and tell them you love them but never get around to it, they may never know how you really feel about them. Good intentions require follow-through and perseverance to become reality and reap rewards.

TODAY'S PLAN

Do you have good intentions for your relationship with God that you have yet to follow through on?

PATIENCE

TODAY'S PROMISE

Patient endurance is what you need now, so that you will continue to do God's will. Then you will receive all that he has promised. —HEBREWS 10:36

TODAY'S THOUGHT

It takes patience to do God's will. In fact, you can't do it without patience because God's will doesn't happen all at once; it unfolds over time. As you pass each test of your faith, you will develop patience for when God asks you to take the next step of faith. Impatience may cause you to rush ahead and take matters into your own hands. At first you trust that God will handle the situation, but when his solution seems slow in coming, you decide that God needs a bit of help. Instead of rushing ahead, you must learn to trust God completely, even if it means having to wait.

TODAY'S PLAN

Do you have the patience to let God's will unfold one day at a time?

COMPETITION

TODAY'S PROMISE

Pay careful attention to your own work, for then you will get the satisfaction of a job well done, and you won't need to compare yourself to anyone else. For we are each responsible for our own conduct.

—GALATIANS 6:4-5

TODAY'S THOUGHT

Competition can be a foothold for pride and jealousy because it often leads you to compare yourself with others. Everyone has equal worth in God's eyes. Anytime you begin to think of yourself as more important or better than others, your competitive spirit is taking you in the wrong direction. When humility tempers your competitive nature, you give everything you have to doing your best, not besting others. Then you will have true satisfaction.

TODAY'S PLAN

Do you experience more personal satisfaction when you do your best or when you do better than others? How can you change your attitude?

WORSHIP

TODAY'S PROMISE

I, the LORD, am holy, and I make you holy.

—LEVITICUS 21:8

God . . . is your example, and you must follow in his steps.

—1 PETER 2:21

TODAY'S THOUGHT

Your character reflects what or whom you worship. For example, a boy who admires his father will try to imitate what his father does. God wants you to have that attitude toward him. God alone should be the object of your worship because he alone is holy, the ultimate example to follow. Through worship, God makes you holy and helps you follow his example in every part of your life. Your character will begin to reflect his character.

TODAY'S PLAN

Does your character reflect God, or something else that you "worship"? How can you make God the only object of your worship?

LONELINESS

TODAY'S PROMISE

The LORD is close to all who call on him, yes, to all who call on him in truth.
— PSALM 145:18

TODAY'S THOUGHT

You may feel alone, but God is always with you. He is thinking about you all the time. He is trying to get your attention. Don't give up on God when you are lonely. Don't abandon all of your relationships because a few have failed. This only causes you to feel sorry for yourself and become discouraged. Use this time of loneliness to discover the faithfulness and presence of God.

TODAY'S PLAN

When you are lonely, do you draw closer to God?

GENTLENESS

TODAY'S PROMISE

Come to me, all of you who are weary and carry heavy burdens, and I will give you rest. Take my yoke upon you. Let me teach you, because I am humble and gentle at heart, and you will find rest for your souls.

—MATTHEW 11:28-29

TODAY'S THOUGHT

In a world full of violence, the concept of gentleness is a welcome one. There is peace in the lives of gentle people that soothes those around them. Businesspeople appreciate a gentle spirit in the office. Church meetings run more smoothly when a spirit of gentleness is present. Jesus was gentle, yet it did not take away from his power or authority. The Bible calls you to be gentle in your dealings with others, not only because it is kind and right but because it promotes peace and gets results.

TODAY'S PLAN

How can you work on developing gentleness?

POTENTIAL

TODAY'S PROMISE

You are the light of the world—like a city on a hilltop that cannot be hidden. . . . Let your good deeds shine out for all to see, so that everyone will praise your heavenly Father.

—MATTHEW 5:14-16

TODAY'S THOUGHT

Have you ever searched for a flashlight, only to discover when you find it that the batteries are dead? Although the flashlight has the potential to provide light, without new batteries it is useless. You, like every believer, have within you the light of Christ and therefore the potential to shine in such a way as to draw others to God. God promises to do amazing things if you let his light shine through you.

TODAY'S PLAN

How can you let God's love shine through you more brightly?

OBEDIENCE

TODAY'S PROMISE

Now that you know these things, God will bless you for doing them. —JOHN 13:17

TODAY'S THOUGHT

Jesus continually warned his listeners about the danger of knowing without doing. You must not only read and hear God's Word; you must also put it into practice. Jesus did not come simply to give you information but to change your life. God will bless your faith in him when you do what he says. As you learn to obey him, you will begin to understand that his way is the best and most satisfying way to live.

TODAY'S PLAN

How often do you let God's commands simply pass through your ears without living them out in a life of obedience?

INTEGRITY

TODAY'S PROMISE

The LORD rewarded me for doing right. He has seen my innocence. To the faithful you show yourself faithful; to those with integrity you show integrity.

—PSALM 18:24-25

TODAY'S THOUGHT

Integrity is essentially the correspondence between your character and the character of God. To develop integrity, your character must become more and more like God's. Just as pure gold is the result of a refining process that purifies the metal and tests it with fire, a life of integrity is the result of a refining process in which you are tested daily to see how pure you are. If God sees that your thoughts and actions are becoming increasingly pure through this testing, then your character is becoming more like his, and you are gradually gaining integrity.

TODAY'S PLAN

Is your character becoming more or less like God's each day?

SPIRITUAL DRYNESS

TODAY'S PROMISE

Oh, the joys of those who do not follow the advice of the wicked, or stand around with sinners, or join in with mockers. . . . They are like trees planted along the riverbank, bearing fruit each season. Their leaves never wither, and they prosper in all they do. —PSALM 1:1-3

TODAY'S THOUGHT

Trees planted along a riverbank receive constant nourishment from the life-giving water that is continually absorbed into the nearby ground. When you plant yourself near the spiritual nourishment of God's Word, you will avoid sin and absorb all the wisdom and blessings of God. You will mature and develop as God's Word feeds you day in and day out.

TODAY'S PLAN

Where do you go to receive spiritual nourishment from God?

SUCCESS

TODAY'S PROMISE

*Commit your actions to the L*ORD*, and your plans will succeed.* —PROVERBS 16:3

TODAY'S THOUGHT

Success according to God's standards is not measured by material assets but by spiritual assets; not by what you have but by who you are; not by what you know but by the God you know. When you die, you will leave behind all material assets and earthly successes because they have absolutely no eternal value. Partnering with God in this life is the best way to ensure success in the next.

TODAY'S PLAN

What kind of success have you been pursuing?

FOLLOWING

TODAY'S PROMISE

Jesus called out to them, "Come, follow me, and I will show you how to fish for people!" And they left their nets at once and followed him. —MATTHEW 4:19-20

TODAY'S THOUGHT

Jesus' invitation to follow him remains a mere opportunity until you decide to accept it. He requires a decision: Follow him or remain where you are. Accepting his invitation leads to action. The disciples stopped what they were doing and followed Jesus. God extends his invitation to you, too. Have you accepted it?

TODAY'S PLAN

Have you accepted Jesus' invitation to follow him?

WORRY

TODAY'S PROMISE

Give your burdens to the LORD, and he will take care of you.

—PSALM 55:22

TODAY'S THOUGHT

When problems and obstacles consume you, you often begin to worry—that you will fail, that you will let others down, that God will not help you when you need him most. When you give in to worry, you focus on the size of your problems rather than on the size of your God. Focus on God instead, and give all your worries to him. He promises that he will take care of you.

TODAY'S PLAN

What is your biggest worry today? How can you give it over to God?

STABILITY

TODAY'S PROMISE

He alone is my rock and my salvation, my fortress where I will never be shaken.
—PSALM 62:2

TODAY'S THOUGHT

Can you lose everything and still have stability in your life? God promises that you can answer yes to this question. He gives you clear principles for finding true stability. Unlike the stock market or interest rates, God never changes, so you know his promises always come true. If you cling only to the stability that this world offers, you will be unsteady and can be shaken by the troubles that will come your way. But if you embrace the eternal and unchanging God, you will stand firm and unshakable throughout your life.

TODAY'S PLAN

What if you lost everything that is most dear to you? Do you have the eternal stability that comes from knowing God?

PLEASURE

TODAY'S PROMISE

You will show me the way of life, granting me the joy of your presence and the pleasures of living with you forever. —PSALM 16:11

TODAY'S THOUGHT

God created you to find pleasure in your relationship with him. The pleasures and blessings that come from knowing him are even more wonderful than the earthly, physical pleasures that God also blesses you with.

TODAY'S PLAN

Do believe that God wants to limit your pleasure or increase it?

LISTENING

TODAY'S PROMISE

Listen to my voice in the morning, LORD. Each morning I bring my requests to you and wait expectantly.
—PSALM 5:3

TODAY'S THOUGHT

God really listens to our prayers, yet so often our prayers lack hope and confidence. God assures you that he is listening when you pray and that he does answer your prayers. When you come to God regularly and expect him to hear and answer, you display your confidence in God's power and participation in your life. Even though he listens, however, he doesn't always indulge you by answering in the way that you want. Expect God to listen, wait for him to answer, and be open to the way he chooses to work.

TODAY'S PLAN

God always listens to you—are you willing to listen to him?

WEAKNESSES

TODAY'S PROMISE

The temptations in your life are no different from what others experience. And God is faithful. He will not allow the temptation to be more than you can stand. When you are tempted, he will show you a way out so that you can endure. —1 CORINTHIANS 10:13

TODAY'S THOUGHT

Your weaknesses are the joints in your spiritual armor at which the enemy takes aim. It is in those areas of weakness where you must ask God to cover your vulnerable spots with his strength. You must understand your weaknesses so you can arm yourself against Satan's attacks. It would be a disaster to discover your weak spots in the heat of the battle; you must discover them before the fighting begins. With God's help and a strategy to protect your points of vulnerability, you will be prepared for any of the enemy's attacks.

TODAY'S PLAN

Are you aware of your weak spots, where Satan will attack you with temptations?

September

LOVE

TODAY'S PROMISE

Nothing can ever separate us from God's love. Neither death nor life, neither angels nor demons, neither our fears for today nor our worries about tomorrow—not even the powers of hell can separate us from God's love. . . . Indeed, nothing in all creation will ever be able to separate us from the love of God that is revealed in Christ Jesus our Lord.

—ROMANS 8:38-39

TODAY'S THOUGHT

One of God's greatest promises is that nothing can separate you from his love. Even your sins cannot keep you from God's love; when you confess them, God clears away your guilt. Though your circumstances will change, you can live confidently because God's love for you never changes.

TODAY'S PLAN

Does the promise of God's love influence the way you live each day?

AMBITION

TODAY'S PROMISE

Wherever there is jealousy and selfish ambition, there you will find disorder and evil of every kind.

—JAMES 3:16

TODAY'S THOUGHT

Ambition is like fire: Both have the potential to be productive or destructive. When a fire is carefully controlled, it produces heat and light. But when a fire rages out of control, it threatens to consume everything in its path. So it is with ambition. Learn to distinguish between godly ambition, which can produce great benefits, and selfish ambition, which can consume and destroy like an uncontained fire. God promises rewards for the first kind of ambition and dire consequences for the other.

TODAY'S PLAN

What is one godly ambition you can pursue today? What is one selfish ambition you can give up?

APPROVAL

TODAY'S PROMISE

The LORD is my light and my salvation—so why should I be afraid? The LORD is my fortress, protecting me from danger, so why should I tremble?

—PSALM 27:1

TODAY'S THOUGHT

Your value is determined by God's approval, not by the approval or disapproval of others. Your ultimate purpose is to please the God who made you and redeemed you, and you can do that no matter what other people may think of you. When you focus on God, you will be able to feel his approval and be less worried about the disapproval you receive from others.

TODAY'S PLAN

Whose approval do you work the hardest to earn? How can you put that energy into your relationship with God?

MONEY

TODAY'S PROMISE

Honor the LORD with your wealth and with the best part of everything you produce. Then he will fill your barns with grain, and your vats will overflow with good wine. —PROVERBS 3:9-10

TODAY'S THOUGHT

Instead of viewing money as yours to use as you wish, see it as God's to use as he wishes. Giving back to God first from everything you receive will help you maintain this perspective, and God promises to bless you because of it.

TODAY'S PLAN

Is giving to God your top financial priority?

LOVE

TODAY'S PROMISE

*The LORD says, "I will rescue those who love me.
I will protect those who trust in my name. When they
call on me, I will answer; I will be with them
in trouble. I will rescue and honor them. I will
reward them with a long life and give them my
salvation."*

—PSALM 91:14-16

TODAY'S THOUGHT

God loves you because he made you. You are
not a creature that randomly evolved from a
prehistoric primordial soup. God created you
in his own image so you could have a relationship
with him. God desires your love and friendship,
and he is courting you now. Accept his love
and discover the purpose for which you were
made.

TODAY'S PLAN

Are you returning God's love?

FREEDOM

TODAY'S PROMISE

The LORD God placed the man in the Garden of Eden to tend and watch over it. But the LORD God warned him, "You may freely eat the fruit of every tree in the garden—except the tree of the knowledge of good and evil. If you eat its fruit, you are sure to die."

—GENESIS 2:15-17

TODAY'S THOUGHT

Genuine love requires the freedom to choose. From the beginning, God desired a loving relationship with you, so he gave you this freedom. If he hadn't given us the freedom to choose, he would have created robots, not humans. But with the ability to make choices comes the possibility that you will choose your own way instead of God's way. Your own way always leads to sin, which breaks God's heart. But you can choose to do right by choosing to follow God's way. When you do so, God is greatly pleased.

TODAY'S PLAN

With your God-given freedom to choose, have you chosen God and his ways?

PASSION

TODAY'S PROMISE

Joyful are those who obey his laws and search for him with all their hearts.

—PSALM 119:2

TODAY'S THOUGHT

If you become excited about something that is not what God wants you to do, your passion for God will quickly die. Sin takes your focus off God and makes it more exciting to pursue something else. Something besides God suddenly gets your attention. The solution to keeping your passion strong is to obey God's commands even when you don't feel like it. This may take a tremendous effort, but intense focus will keep you from becoming apathetic. Whatever takes great effort stimulates and engages you, and this ignites your passion for God.

TODAY'S PLAN

Has anything become more exciting to you than following God? How can you renew your passion for him?

BUSINESS

TODAY'S PROMISE

Good comes to those who lend money generously and conduct their business fairly.

—PSALM 112:5

TODAY'S THOUGHT

God gives us advice about business because that's where so many people spend the most productive hours of their day. Even though you probably can't choose much of what you have to do during the day, you can choose who you are and how you react. That will impact your work far more than you realize. God promises that your greatest fulfillment will come when you focus on filling needs and serving God as your ultimate bottom line.

TODAY'S PLAN

What principles are you using to conduct yourself at work?

CONSCIENCE

TODAY'S PROMISE

Be careful. Don't let your heart be deceived so that you turn away from the LORD and serve and worship other gods. If you do, the LORD's anger will burn against you.

—DEUTERONOMY 11:16-17

TODAY'S THOUGHT

When you sin, you are deliberately going against your conscience. You know what you are doing is wrong because your conscience tells you it is, but you do it anyway because sin is often so appealing. If you continually do what your conscience tells you not to, eventually you will no longer hear it warning you of danger. Without a strong conscience, you become desensitized to sin and your heart becomes hardened. The key to a healthy conscience is faith in Jesus Christ.

TODAY'S PLAN

Have you been listening to your conscience or ignoring it? Your answer may be an indication of the condition of your faith.

ACCOMPLISHMENTS

TODAY'S PROMISE

This Good News tells us how God makes us right in his sight. This is accomplished from start to finish by faith. As the Scriptures say, "It is through faith that a righteous person has life." —ROMANS 1:17

TODAY'S THOUGHT

Salvation is truly the greatest of accomplishments, but ironically it is not accomplished through your own work—it only comes through the work of God in your heart. Salvation is simply a matter of faith, of believing that Jesus Christ died for your sins so that you can live forever with him in heaven. Thank God for accomplishing this tremendous work in you!

TODAY'S PLAN

What can you accomplish today because of God's work of salvation in you?

ADVERSITY

TODAY'S PROMISE

When you go through deep waters, I will be with you. When you go through rivers of difficulty, you will not drown. When you walk through the fire of oppression, you will not be burned up; the flames will not consume you. For I am the LORD, your God . . . your Savior.

—ISAIAH 43:2-3

TODAY'S THOUGHT

When you face great adversity, you may ask, "Where is God now, when I need him most?" The answer is always the same—he is right beside you. God is there, and he has the power to help you. God doesn't promise to save you from trouble in this life. Instead, he promises to be with you in your troubles and give you endurance, strength, and understanding as you learn to deal with adversity.

TODAY'S PLAN

The next time adversity overwhelms you, focus on how God will help you through it.

GUILT

TODAY'S PROMISE

Finally, I confessed all my sins to you and stopped trying to hide my guilt. I said to myself, "I will confess my rebellion to the LORD." And you forgave me! All my guilt is gone. —PSALM 32:5

TODAY'S THOUGHT

Guilt over sin is actually a good thing because it shows that your conscience is working properly. It is appropriate to feel guilty when you have done something wrong, to genuinely feel bad that you have hurt God and let him down. Until you ask Jesus to forgive you, you will suffer from the guilt lurking inside you. But confession and forgiveness remove both the sin and the guilt and give you a fresh start with God. No matter how often you fail God, he will always forgive you. You don't need to feel guilty anymore because God has already forgotten your sin!

TODAY'S PLAN

Are you overwhelmed by a guilty conscience? Have you allowed God to forgive you and take your guilt away?

CONFIDENCE

TODAY'S PROMISE

The LORD keeps watch over you as you come and go, both now and forever.

—PSALM 121:8

TODAY'S THOUGHT

Many great athletes say that the biggest obstacle to winning is mental, not physical. It's the same way in your spiritual life. Your confidence does not come from your physical circumstances—how you look or what you achieve. Rather, it comes from faith—the inner assurance that God is by your side, daily protecting you, fighting for you, and winning the victories in your life for you.

TODAY'S PLAN

What can you do to increase your confidence that God is actively involved in your life?

PLANS

TODAY'S PROMISE

You can make many plans, but the LORD's purpose will prevail.
—PROVERBS 19:21

TODAY'S THOUGHT

It is not that planning is futile. Rather, the promise for today gives you the good news that your plans cannot mess up God's plans. His plans will ultimately prevail. And if you are following him, you are part of his good plans!

TODAY'S PLAN

Are your plans carrying out God's plans, or is God working his will despite your plans?

COURAGE

TODAY'S PROMISE

Don't be afraid, for I am with you. Don't be discouraged, for I am your God. I will strengthen you and help you. I will hold you up with my victorious right hand.

—ISAIAH 41:10

TODAY'S THOUGHT

Over the course of your lifetime, you and those you lead will face many frightening situations— mortal danger, extreme stress, major illness, financial hardships, any number of problems. True courage comes from understanding that God is stronger than your biggest problem or your worst enemy and wants you to use his power. Courage is not misplaced confidence in your own strength; it is well-placed confidence in God's strength. Fear comes from feeling alone against a great threat, but courage comes from knowing that God is beside you, helping you fight.

TODAY'S PLAN

What major problem do you need the courage to face today? Can you sense God's presence beside you?

CRISIS

TODAY'S PROMISE

Call on me when you are in trouble, and I will rescue you, and you will give me glory. —PSALM 50:15

TODAY'S THOUGHT

We are most severely tested in times of crisis because there are so many things out of our control. Allow crisis to become a means for God to rescue you, to reveal his care and his power working on your behalf.

TODAY'S PLAN

Can the people around you see that you trust God in times of crisis?

BACKSLIDING

TODAY'S PROMISE

Come back to me and live!
— AMOS 5:4

Keep watch and pray, so that you will not give in to temptation. For the spirit is willing, but the body is weak!
— MATTHEW 26:41

TODAY'S THOUGHT

Backsliding is taking a step backward in your spiritual walk with God, falling back into a sinful lifestyle or habit. It weakens your relationship with God. Each time you backslide, you become more comfortable with your old, sinful habit. Your heart becomes a little bit harder, making it more difficult for you to hear God calling you back to him. But each time you obey God's Word, each time you pray, each time you remind yourself to be alert to temptation, you will be taking a step toward God instead of away from him. It simply takes discipline and practice to keep from backsliding.

TODAY'S PLAN

How can you learn to listen to God and avoid backsliding?

IDOLATRY

TODAY'S PROMISE

Say this to those who worship other gods: "Your so-called gods, who did not make the heavens and earth, will vanish from the earth and from under the heavens."

—JEREMIAH 10:11

TODAY'S THOUGHT

It's easier to count on something or someone you can see. But if you count on it too much, it might become an object of worship. The Bible calls this idolatry. We all have idols—a sports team, stock portfolio, job, house, electronic gadget, a hobby—and the more we focus on things, the less we focus on God. The Bible promises that things will eventually vanish. But the God we can't see will last forever, and in heaven he'll be more real than anything we could imagine. There's nothing wrong with enjoying things, but it's wrong when those things replace God as the object of our affection.

TODAY'S PLAN

What are the idols in your life?

HUMILITY

TODAY'S PROMISE

Humble yourselves before the Lord, and he will lift you up in honor.
—JAMES 4:10

TODAY'S THOUGHT

Humility is essential for recognizing sin in your life. Pride gives the devil the key to your heart, but humility gives God your whole heart. In place of pride, you need the humility that comes from true sorrow over sin. Humility allows you to openly admit that you need God and ask for his forgiveness—something that no proud person could do. When you give your whole heart to God, you open yourself up to being used by him at just the right time and place.

TODAY'S PLAN

Do you recognize sin in your life? If so, you are developing a humble heart.

COMFORT

TODAY'S PROMISE

He comforts us in all our troubles so that we can comfort others. When they are troubled, we will be able to give them the same comfort God has given us.

—2 CORINTHIANS 1:4

TODAY'S THOUGHT

There are two things to remember about suffering. First, it hurts. Second, it helps when others bring you comfort. Your suffering gives you the life experience you need to comfort others. When you join in someone else's suffering, you are choosing to feel their pain with them. This woundedness may appear to weaken you, but it actually makes you stronger. If you know someone who is hurting, suffer along with that person to bring them comfort and hope.

TODAY'S PLAN

Do you know someone who needs comfort? How can you suffer with that person?

ROMANCE

TODAY'S PROMISE

Surely your goodness and unfailing love will pursue me all the days of my life, and I will live in the house of the LORD forever.

—PSALM 23:6

TODAY'S THOUGHT

Romance is the language of love that fosters intimacy with another person. What a wonderful feeling when someone expresses their affection for you, enjoys your company, and is captivated by you! As you read the Bible, you learn that God himself is a romantic who desires an intimate relationship with you. He desires your company and is interested in the smallest details of your life. He wants nothing more than to walk with you through this life and for eternity. As you realize how precious and valuable you are to God, you will find confidence in your faith, strength to be faithful to him, and a deep desire to know him better.

TODAY'S PLAN

What can you learn from God about romance and love? Where's the romance in your faith?

SALVATION

TODAY'S PROMISE

Since our friendship with God was restored by the death of his Son while we were still his enemies, we will certainly be saved through the life of his Son. —ROMANS 5:10

TODAY'S THOUGHT

Sin separates you from God. As long as you are separated from him, you cannot experience a relationship with him. That is why God sent his Son, Jesus, to die in your place. He took the punishment for your sins so you wouldn't have to. Jesus' resurrection from the dead proves his power over death and sin and gives you complete assurance that you will have eternal life with him. When you believe that Jesus died for your sins and was raised from the dead, when you confess your sins and ask God to forgive you, and when you commit yourself to obeying him, God gives you his salvation and restores you to fellowship with him, both now and forever.

TODAY'S PLAN

Do you live like you've been restored to fellowship with God?

TEMPTATION

TODAY'S PROMISE

Even Satan disguises himself as an angel of light. So it is no wonder that his servants also disguise themselves as servants of righteousness. In the end they will get the punishment their wicked deeds deserve.

—2 CORINTHIANS 11:14-15

TODAY'S THOUGHT

One of Satan's favorite strategies is to make sin look desirable and good and to convince you that what is true is actually false. He is the master of disguise and deception. He tries to trick you into believing that if it feels right, it must be right; that pleasure is always good; that truth is whatever works for you. Don't buy into Satan's deceptions, or you will face the same eternal fate. When you are tempted to think something is right because it feels right to you, check it against the standard of God's Word to make sure it isn't Satan in disguise.

TODAY'S PLAN

How can you get better at seeing through Satan's disguises and resisting his temptations?

SURRENDER

TODAY'S PROMISE

If you try to hang on to your life, you will lose it. But if you give up your life for my sake, you will save it.

—MATTHEW 16:25

TODAY'S THOUGHT

God promises that you will gain more if you give something up. When you give up your own agenda and give up your soul to God, you will gain eternal life and eternal rewards. You will also gain a sense of peace and security that you could never have otherwise.

TODAY'S PLAN

What do you need to give up in order to gain God's promise to save your life?

PERSPECTIVE

TODAY'S PROMISE

When the Great Shepherd appears, you will receive a crown of never-ending glory and honor. . . . In his kindness God called you to share in his eternal glory by means of Christ Jesus. So after you have suffered a little while, he will restore, support, and strengthen you, and he will place you on a firm foundation.

—1 PETER 5:4, 10

TODAY'S THOUGHT

As a heaven-bound follower of Jesus, try to put earth and heaven in perspective. Here, you will probably live for less than a hundred years. In heaven, one hundred *million* years will be just the beginning. If you are going to spend most of your time in heaven, you should spend your time here on earth preparing yourself to live there. Having an eternal perspective will help you live today with the right priorities, for this life is really your preparation for eternity.

TODAY'S PLAN

How can an eternal perspective change the way you live today?

MOTIVES

TODAY'S PROMISE

People may be right in their own eyes, but the LORD examines their heart.

—PROVERBS 21:2

TODAY'S THOUGHT

When someone gives a thousand dollars to a charity, it seems like such a good and selfless act. But one person may do it in order to earn a tax break; another may do it to win political favor; another person may, in fact, do it out of deep compassion for the poor. The same act can be set in motion by very different motives. The Bible teaches that God is as interested in our motives as he is in our behavior. Selfish and sinful motives eventually produce selfish and sinful behavior, but good and godly motives result in true good works.

TODAY'S PLAN

Evaluate every decision you make today. How many of your actions are based on good motives rather than selfish ones?

SIN

TODAY'S PROMISE

*He personally carried our sins in his body on the cross
so that we can be dead to sin and live for what is right.
By his wounds you are healed.* —1 PETER 2:24

TODAY'S THOUGHT

Sin is a disease of the soul that will eventually
destroy you if you don't treat it. Ironically, the
antidote for sin not only costs you nothing,
but it also comes with the free gift of eternal
life. The fact that such a bargain from God is
so hard to accept shows just how enticing and
enslaving sin can be. To be "dead to sin" doesn't
mean that you won't sin anymore in this life; it
means you will no longer be completely controlled by sin. You will begin to want to please
God and do what is right.

TODAY'S PLAN

Are you sick with sin or alive in Christ?

HELP

TODAY'S PROMISE

With God's help we will do mighty things.

—PSALM 60:12

TODAY'S THOUGHT

If we ask God only for protection and success, we're not asking him for nearly enough. Most of our requests stop with us and therefore fall short of our potential. Don't ask God to help you just for the sake of you receiving help. Ask him to help you so you can accomplish something great for him.

TODAY'S PLAN

What might happen if you asked God for the kind of help that would reach beyond yourself and accomplish great things?

CHURCH

TODAY'S PROMISE

God has put all things under the authority of Christ and has made him head over all things for the benefit of the church. And the church is his body; it is made full and complete by Christ, who fills all things everywhere with himself. —EPHESIANS 1:22-23

TODAY'S THOUGHT

God wants to do great things through the church. The people of God are filled with Jesus himself and are his representatives to the world. When you and other believers come together under the headship of Christ, you can have the confidence that God will be at work for the good of his church and the world. With his help, the church can do more than you ever could have imagined.

TODAY'S PLAN

How can you become more involved in the great things God is doing through the church?

CIRCUMSTANCES

TODAY'S PROMISE

Light shines in the darkness for the godly. They are generous, compassionate, and righteous. . . . Such people will not be overcome by evil. Those who are righteous will be long remembered. They do not fear bad news; they confidently trust the LORD to care for them. They are confident and fearless and can face their foes triumphantly. —PSALM 112:4, 6-8

TODAY'S THOUGHT

Sometimes we don't feel like God is with us in our day-to-day circumstances. But if God went to such great trouble to create us and the world we live in, to send his Son to die for our sins and prepare an eternal home for us in heaven, wouldn't he also want to be involved in every detail of our lives? Watch closely for God's presence and power at work in your past, present, and future. Pray for his intervention in your life, and wait confidently for his answer and his help.

TODAY'S PLAN

How can you learn to see God at work in your everyday circumstances?

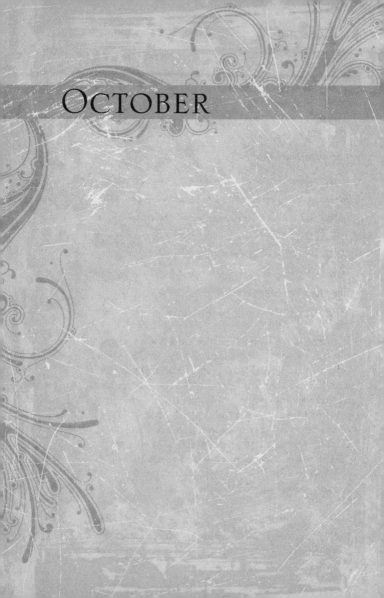

OCTOBER

NEEDS

Enjoy what you have rather than desiring what you don't have. —ECCLESIASTES 6:9

Seek the Kingdom of God above all else, and he will give you everything you need. —LUKE 12:31

TODAY'S THOUGHT

When you don't get what you want—or what you think you need—think of it as an opportunity for God to give you what he wants for you. When you align your priorities with God's, you begin to enjoy what he has already given you. In fact, you will likely discover that he has given you everything you truly need.

TODAY'S PLAN

Do you think your list of needs matches up with what God knows you need?

COMPROMISE

TODAY'S PROMISE

If the godly give in to the wicked, it's like polluting a fountain or muddying a spring. —PROVERBS 25:26

TODAY'S THOUGHT

There's a difference between flexibility and compromise. Flexibility is adapting to changing circumstances. Compromise is giving in to what opposes God. Be careful not to bend too far and break the laws of God. Then you would pollute your soul with sin and make it harder to hold on to your convictions the next time you are tempted to compromise.

TODAY'S PLAN

Are there any areas in your faith where you are compromising for the sake of flexibility?

SORROW

TODAY'S PROMISE

How long must I struggle with anguish in my soul, with sorrow in my heart every day? . . . Turn and answer me, O LORD my God! Restore the sparkle to my eyes, or I will die.   —PSALM 13:2-3

TODAY'S THOUGHT

When you feel overwhelmed by sorrow, it is easy to turn inward and become paralyzed by your sadness and pain. Though it may take some effort, you need to refocus your attention outward, on God. Every day he opens doors of opportunity that can bring you new purpose and meaning: helping someone in need, volunteering for a good cause, writing a note of encouragement to someone in worse circumstances than your own. When you lift your gaze from the ground, you will see the door God has opened for you. Walk through it with courage, and on the other side you will find relief from your sorrow.

TODAY'S PLAN

Are you ready to look up from your sorrow and see how God wants to help you?

SECURITY

TODAY'S PROMISE

All praise to God, the Father of our Lord Jesus Christ, who has blessed us with every spiritual blessing in the heavenly realms because we are united with Christ.

—EPHESIANS 1:3

TODAY'S THOUGHT

No enemy or adversity can ever take away your most important blessings—your relationship with God, his forgiveness of your sins, eternal life with him. These remain secure even when your world falls apart and everything else is taken away from you.

TODAY'S PLAN

Your spiritual blessings are your most secure blessings; are they also the most important?

EMOTIONS

TODAY'S PROMISE

The Holy Spirit produces this kind of fruit in our lives: love, joy, peace, patience, kindness, goodness, faithfulness, gentleness, and self-control. —GALATIANS 5:22-23

TODAY'S THOUGHT

We often think of emotions negatively because they tend to get out of control. But without emotions, you could not experience the power and satisfaction of a relationship with God, nor could you model the character of God in your life. Don't deny your emotions, but don't let them control you or cause you to sin. Allow the emotions God has given you to deepen your relationship with him. They will help you experience the drama and power of the Christian life.

TODAY'S PLAN

Which emotions help you feel closer to God?

STRENGTH

TODAY'S PROMISE

God has not given us a spirit of fear and timidity, but of power, love, and self-discipline. —2 TIMOTHY 1:7

I also pray that you will understand the incredible greatness of God's power for us who believe him. This is the same mighty power that raised Christ from the dead. —EPHESIANS 1:19-20

TODAY'S THOUGHT

When you realize that you can tap into the same power that raised Jesus from the dead, you will be able to experience more of God's strength in your life. God promises to infuse you with his strength when you depend on him. Each morning, ask him to give you strength for the day. You will experience a power for living that you never thought possible!

TODAY'S PLAN

Do you really believe that God's strength is available to you today?

WORK

TODAY'S PROMISE

Work willingly at whatever you do, as though you were working for the Lord rather than for people. Remember that the Lord will give you an inheritance as your reward, and that the Master you are serving is Christ.
—COLOSSIANS 3:23-24

TODAY'S THOUGHT

If you have a really great supervisor, you probably find it easy to go the extra mile to please him or her. You may not often think about Jesus being your Master, but he is—not just at work, but in all areas of your life. He promises to reward those who work hard. Your reward could be financial, but not necessarily. It will definitely include gaining respect and personal satisfaction, bringing honor to God, and finding joy in contributing to the needs of others, not to mention receiving an eternal inheritance. The Lord of your life is truly worth going the extra mile for!

TODAY'S PLAN

Do you ever think of Jesus as your supervisor?

QUITTING

TODAY'S PROMISE

Since Christ suffered physical pain, you must arm yourselves with the same attitude he had, and be ready to suffer, too. For if you have suffered physically for Christ, you have finished with sin.
—1 PETER 4:1

TODAY'S THOUGHT

Sometimes it is wise to quit, such as when you are doing something wrong, when you realize that your actions are futile, or when you are hurting someone. But when God has called you to a task, you should not give up. The fact that God asks you to do something doesn't mean it will be easy. In fact, the more important the task, the harder it often is. If you know God is calling you to a certain task or taking you in a new direction, don't give up just because the going gets tough. If anything, your suffering tells you that you are headed in the right direction.

TODAY'S PLAN

How can you know when to quit and when to keep going?

OVERWHELMED

TODAY'S PROMISE

The LORD helps the fallen and lifts those bent beneath their loads.
                                        —PSALM 145:14

All praise to God, the Father of our Lord Jesus Christ. God is our merciful Father and the source of all comfort.
                                        —2 CORINTHIANS 1:3

TODAY'S THOUGHT

Today's promises assure you of two important truths: God notices when you are overloaded and overwhelmed, and he provides you with an extra measure of mercy, comfort, and help when you need it most. When you are overwhelmed, don't shut God out; let him in so he can help you.

TODAY'S PLAN

How do you cope when life gets overwhelming?

WITNESSING

TODAY'S PROMISE

When you are brought to trial in the synagogues and before rulers and authorities, don't worry about how to defend yourself or what to say, for the Holy Spirit will teach you at that time what needs to be said.

—LUKE 12:11-12

TODAY'S THOUGHT

Even the boldest witnesses find themselves in situations where it is difficult or even dangerous to share their faith. God promises that you can call on him for courage to speak the truth confidently, and he will give you the right words to speak. The effectiveness of God's message does not depend on the eloquence of your own speech but on the power of the living God communicating through you. God is the One who touches people's hearts, and he promises to do so through the words of willing witnesses.

TODAY'S PLAN

The next time you need to speak up and give witness of your faith, can you trust God to speak through you?

SPIRITUAL GIFTS

TODAY'S PROMISE

There are different kinds of spiritual gifts, but the same Spirit is the source of them all. There are different kinds of service, but we serve the same Lord. God works in different ways, but it is the same God who does the work in all of us. A spiritual gift is given to each of us so we can help each other.

—1 CORINTHIANS 12:4-7

TODAY'S THOUGHT

The natural abilities you have are gifts from God, and they are often a clue to what God wants you to do. You may have natural gifts in the area of leadership, public speaking, managing a business, teaching, handling money, fixing or building things, or any number of other areas. Use whatever gifts you have been given to bring honor and glory to God. Then you will be right where you need to be to discover God's will for you and to accomplish the purpose for which he created you.

TODAY'S PLAN

How is God calling you to serve him with your gifts?

FREEDOM

TODAY'S PROMISE

The LORD will redeem those who serve him. No one who takes refuge in him will be condemned. —PSALM 34:22

I will walk in freedom, for I have devoted myself to your commandments.
                                                              —PSALM 119:45

TODAY'S THOUGHT

Being a servant of God is true freedom because your relationship with him liberates you from the sin, burdens, and temptations that enslave you in this life. Being a servant of God lifts your death sentence and takes away your guilt so you can live freely, having the confidence that nothing can take away your eternal life and salvation.

TODAY'S PLAN

Now that you are no longer a slave to sin, are you content to be a servant of God?

RENEWAL

TODAY'S PROMISE

That is why we never give up. Though our bodies are dying, our spirits are being renewed every day.

—2 CORINTHIANS 4:16

TODAY'S THOUGHT

We often have high hopes and pure intentions, but inevitably we find ourselves weary and burned out, victims of self-defeat or bad circumstances. The messiness of life can leave you feeling exhausted, not only physically but spiritually as well. When you get to this point, you are in desperate need of renewal. Renewal begins with God's compassion and your own desire for change. When the two are brought together, you will find a new beginning, a soul refreshed, and a life revived.

TODAY'S PLAN

How might God bring renewal into your life today if you let him?

TESTING

TODAY'S PROMISE

God blesses those who patiently endure testing and temptation. Afterward they will receive the crown of life that God has promised to those who love him. And remember, when you are being tempted, do not say, "God is tempting me." God is never tempted to do wrong, and he never tempts anyone else.

—JAMES 1:12-13

TODAY'S THOUGHT

The Bible distinguishes between temptation, which Satan uses to lead you into sin, and testing, which God uses to purify you and help you grow and mature. Satan tempts you in order to destroy you. He wants you to fail and miss out on eternity with God. But God tests you for your own good. He wants you to succeed, to pass each test and receive his rewards, both in this life and in eternity. He promises to reward you when you endure testing.

TODAY'S PLAN

Do you think God is testing you in some way? How might you grow stronger as you endure his testing?

LOVE

TODAY'S PROMISE

You were cleansed from your sins when you obeyed the truth, so now you must show sincere love to each other as brothers and sisters. Love each other deeply with all your heart.
—1 PETER 1:22

TODAY'S THOUGHT

Because of God's love, you are given the free gift of salvation even though you don't deserve it. Because of God's mercy, you are forgiven and freed from guilt. Because of God's kindness, you will have a place in heaven for all eternity. When you realize how desperately you need God's love and mercy, you will understand the importance of showing love and mercy to others.

TODAY'S PLAN

Do you recognize your own need for God's love and mercy?

RESPONSIBILITY

TODAY'S PROMISE

To those who use well what they are given, even more will be given, and they will have an abundance.

—MATTHEW 25:29

TODAY'S THOUGHT

It seems that no one wants to take responsibility for their actions; nothing is ever "my fault." But God promises that if you take responsibility for your actions and use well what he has given you, he will give you more opportunities and more blessings. In the end, each person will be responsible for his own decisions, behavior, and relationships. Ultimately, everyone is responsible to God. Show responsibility in how you use the gifts and opportunities God has given you, and he will reward you.

TODAY'S PLAN

Are you taking responsibility for everything God has given you?

RISK

TODAY'S PROMISE

When you work in a quarry, stones might fall and crush you. When you chop wood, there is danger with each stroke of your ax. —ECCLESIASTES 10:9

Do not be afraid of the terrors of the night, nor the arrow that flies in the day. Do not dread the disease that stalks in darkness, nor the disaster that strikes at midday. —PSALM 91:5-6

TODAY'S THOUGHT

Life is filled with risks. The person who never takes any risks never succeeds, never enjoys everything life has to offer, and never fully experiences God's plan. You are too cautious if you let fear control you to the point where any risk seems too great. Fear keeps you from taking risks at all. Caution keeps you from risking too much. Obedience to God balances the two. When you move forward in obedience to God, you experience the privilege of watching him at work as he works through you.

TODAY'S PLAN

Do you need to take more risks to obey God?

CARELESSNESS

TODAY'S PROMISE

I listen carefully to what God the LORD is saying, for he speaks peace to his faithful people. But let them not return to their foolish ways. —PSALM 85:8

TODAY'S THOUGHT

Carelessness in your relationship with God will lead to disobedience. You become careless about sin and the way you live before your holy God. The opposite of being careless is being careful. Be careful with your thoughts, words, and actions. Be careful to listen to and obey God's Word. Then you will have peace and a deeper intimacy with God.

TODAY'S PLAN

Have you grown careless in your relationship with God?

STRESS

TODAY'S PROMISE

I will call to you whenever I'm in trouble, and you will answer me. —PSALM 86:7

TODAY'S THOUGHT

Stress can put tremendous pressure on your health and your relationships. It can stretch you to your limit until you feel as if you will snap. But stress can be positive if you learn to grow from it. Just as your muscles grow only when pushed beyond their limits, your faith grows only when stretched by the pressures of life. When you call upon God in stressful times, he promises to answer you and equip you to deal with stress in the future.

TODAY'S PLAN

How can you see stress as positive?

ACCOMPLISHMENTS

TODAY'S PROMISE

God is not unjust. He will not forget how hard you have worked for him and how you have shown your love to him by caring for other believers, as you still do.

—HEBREWS 6:10

TODAY'S THOUGHT

There is a difference between accomplishing things to earn God's love and accomplishing things to show your love for him. When you stop trying to impress God with your accomplishments, you will be able to trust and enjoy his gracious gift of love. This will allow you to love him and others without expecting anything in return. God embraces you not for how much you have done but for who you are.

TODAY'S PLAN

Do you love in order to earn something for yourself? Or do you love simply because God first loved you?

ASSUMPTIONS

TODAY'S PROMISE

Don't just say to each other, "We're safe."

—MATTHEW 3:9

There is only one God, and he makes people right with himself only by faith, whether they are Jews or Gentiles.

—ROMANS 3:30

TODAY'S THOUGHT

Don't just assume you will go to heaven. The Bible says the only way to heaven is through faith in Jesus Christ, God's Son. When you believe in the truth of Jesus' life, death, and resurrection, you are able to have a relationship with God. He sends the Holy Spirit to live within you to help you live out your faith and produce spiritual fruit. You then have the assurance—not just the assumption—that you belong to God and will spend eternity with him in heaven.

TODAY'S PLAN

Are you certain that you're going to heaven?

BALANCE

TODAY'S PROMISE

I brought glory to you here on earth by completing the work you gave me to do. —JOHN 17:4-5

TODAY'S THOUGHT

God assures you there is time for everything he calls you to do. Jesus, despite his power and the needs of those around him, left much undone; yet he completed everything God had planned for him to do. You will find true peace and contentment when you realize you don't have to do everything, just those things God wants you to do. Then you can leave some things undone, knowing that in God's eyes you have done everything you need to.

TODAY'S PLAN

How do you spend most of your time? Do you have enough time to do the things God has called you to do?

TRAINING

TODAY'S PROMISE

Physical training is good, but training for godliness is much better, promising benefits in this life and in the life to come. —1 TIMOTHY 4:8

TODAY'S THOUGHT

Physical training is a good model for the kind of training required to become spiritually healthy. If you want to be physically healthy, you must develop good habits: eating right, exercising, and getting proper rest. If you want to be spiritually healthy, you must also develop good habits: feeding on God's Word; exercising the spiritual disciplines of prayer, meditation, and worship; and finding rest and peace in God's care and promises.

TODAY'S PLAN

Do you have a spiritual-training plan?

POWER

TODAY'S PROMISE

It is not that we think we are qualified to do anything on our own. Our qualification comes from God.

—2 CORINTHIANS 3:5

TODAY'S THOUGHT

Power is intoxicating; with it comes recognition, control, and often wealth. These can feed pride, and pride leads us away from God and into sin. This is why power so often corrupts. If you are in a position of power or authority, two things will help you use it wisely: accountability and service. When you have to explain your motives to others, you will be more careful about what you do and say. And when you serve others instead of yourself with your power, you will gain support and loyalty from the people in your care.

TODAY'S PLAN

How are you using your power?

CONSISTENCY

TODAY'S PROMISE

Keep on doing what is right, and trust your lives to the God who created you, for he will never fail you.

—1 PETER 4:19

TODAY'S THOUGHT

If you drift away from consistent obedience to God, you will lose your eternal perspective of why obedience is important. Your daily choices will become selfish, and you will begin to feel cynical and dissatisfied. Keep on doing what is right, and God promises to bless you.

TODAY'S PLAN

How can you obey God more consistently?

SIN

TODAY'S PROMISE

Even if we feel guilty, God is greater than our feelings, and he knows everything. —1 JOHN 3:20

Those who look to him for help will be radiant with joy; no shadow of shame will darken their faces.
—PSALM 34:5

TODAY'S THOUGHT

The light of God's Word brings you face-to-face with the darkness of sin overshadowing your heart. Some sins you are all too familiar with, and others you have committed unknowingly. Confession shines the bright light of God's forgiveness into these dark corners of your heart, exposing them and cleansing them. As long as you keep God's light in your heart, there will be no dark areas for sin to live.

TODAY'S PLAN

Is the light of God's Word shining brightly in your heart?

HEALING

TODAY'S PROMISE

A man with leprosy came and knelt in front of Jesus, begging to be healed. "If you are willing, you can heal me and make me clean," he said. Moved with compassion, Jesus reached out and touched him. "I am willing," he said. "Be healed!" Instantly the leprosy disappeared, and the man was healed.

—MARK 1:40-42

TODAY'S THOUGHT

When Jesus touched the leper, he revealed both God's power and compassion for the whole person. God can and does heal people today— through the body's natural processes, medical science, and miraculous means. Jesus also heals the disease of sin, through forgiveness and grace. Don't be afraid to ask for his healing.

TODAY'S PLAN

Has Jesus healed the sin in your life?

PRAYER

TODAY'S PROMISE

We are confident that he hears us whenever we ask for anything that pleases him. —1 JOHN 5:14

TODAY'S THOUGHT

While you may not know God's specific will for every situation in your life, you can be sure he wants to empower you to obey him, to help you overcome evil with good, and to equip you to do his work in the world. You can pray confidently for his power and guidance in these things that please him, and in many others, knowing that you are asking for the things he most longs to give you.

TODAY'S PLAN

Do you regularly ask God for the things he wants to give you?

SURRENDER

TODAY'S PROMISE

*You cannot become my disciple without giving up
everything you own.* —LUKE 14:33

TODAY'S THOUGHT

Jesus is not saying that you *must* give up everything
to follow him but that you must be *willing* to.
Only when you are willing to give up everything
for God will you be able to receive everything
he wants to offer you. We often foolishly fight
against God and his will for us because we want
to have ultimate control over our lives. But surrender is necessary. You surrender to God when
you realize you are powerless against sin and you
give control of your life to God. Then you will
truly be a disciple of Jesus.

TODAY'S PLAN

Are you willing to give up everything for God?

FATIGUE

TODAY'S PROMISE

He gives power to the weak and strength to the powerless. Even youths will become weak and tired, and young men will fall in exhaustion. But those who trust in the LORD will find new strength. They will soar high on wings like eagles. They will run and not grow weary. They will walk and not faint.

—ISAIAH 40:29-31

TODAY'S THOUGHT

Fatigue can make you more vulnerable to temptation and danger. When you are weary, it is so easy to give in to what tempts you. Tap into God's power by reading the Bible and praying, and you will find strength you never thought you had. God's Word is not some fable or fairy tale; it offers real, supernatural power from the One who created you and sustains you.

TODAY'S PLAN

Are you ready to rely on God and discover the benefits of his strength?

JOY

TODAY'S PROMISE

Praise the LORD! How joyful are those who fear the LORD and delight in obeying his commands.

—PSALM 112:1

TODAY'S THOUGHT

Doesn't it seem ironic that the more you fear the Lord, the more joyful you will be? But the Bible says that to fear the Lord—to respect him so much you want to listen to what he says—is the way to obedience. Obedience helps you make good choices that bring joy and happiness, and it helps you avoid harmful choices that bring misery.

TODAY'S PLAN

Are you making the kind of choices that will bring joy?

NOVEMBER

PATIENCE

TODAY'S PROMISE

This vision is for a future time. . . . If it seems slow in coming, wait patiently, for it will surely take place. It will not be delayed. —HABAKKUK 2:3

TODAY'S THOUGHT

Sometimes we lose patience with God. We become restless and bored while we wait for his plans to be fulfilled in our lives. Patiently waiting for God can actually help you anticipate each new day. God is doing what is best for you, so his plan will be accomplished on his schedule, not yours. Keeping that in mind, you can actually become excited about waiting for him to act. You awake each day anticipating what good thing he will accomplish in your life, and it will be just right for you at just the right time.

TODAY'S PLAN

How can you get excited about patiently waiting for God?

MEANING

TODAY'S PROMISE

Bring all who claim me as their God, for I have made them for my glory. It was I who created them.

—ISAIAH 43:7

TODAY'S THOUGHT

A primary cause of despair is the feeling that life is ultimately meaningless. Why keep going if nothing really matters? Conversely, the sense that life has meaning gives a person energy, purpose, and resilience, even in the midst of trials. God, as your Creator, gives you value, and he promises that your life matters to him. You are made in his image, and his very breath has given you life. You are created to know God and enjoy fellowship with him. What could be more meaningful than a relationship with your Creator?

TODAY'S PLAN

How does being made in God's image bring meaning into your life?

FINDING GOD

Anyone who wants to come to him must believe that God exists and that he rewards those who sincerely seek him.
—HEBREWS 11:6

You won't find God or see the evidence of his work in your life if you don't believe he actually exists or don't give him the time of day. If you don't sincerely work at developing a relationship with him, how can you expect him to bless and reward you? If you never look for God or if you lose sight of him, you will be in danger of denying his existence and experiencing judgment rather than blessing. But if you seek after God, he promises that you will find him and experience his presence and rewards.

Have you found God? If not, are you sincerely looking for him?

FORGIVENESS

TODAY'S PROMISE

O Lord, you are so good, so ready to forgive, so full of unfailing love for all who ask for your help. —PSALM 86:5

TODAY'S THOUGHT

Forgiveness requires two parties—one to ask for it and the other to give it. Between you and God, you are always on the asking side, and he is always on the giving side. If you are sincere, you are assured of God's forgiveness. No matter what mistakes you've made, God promises that he will completely remove the stain of your sins. When God forgives, he doesn't simply sweep your sins under the carpet; he completely washes them away.

TODAY'S PLAN

Have you asked for God's forgiveness?

HAPPINESS

TODAY'S PROMISE

I know the LORD is always with me. . . . He is right beside me. No wonder my heart is glad, and I rejoice.

—PSALM 16:8-9

TODAY'S THOUGHT

Is happiness merely a passing emotion, or is it a permanent state of being? The Bible says it can be both. There is happiness that is a reaction to happenings, which is temporary and volatile; and there is happiness that is above and beyond happenings, which is strong and lasting. If happiness based on happenings is all we have, we must keep finding good things and good experiences to keep us happy. Those who know the joy that comes from God don't need experiences to keep them happy. They have inner joy because they know that no matter what happens, God is with them and promises lasting hope and happiness.

TODAY'S PLAN

Are you looking in the right place for lasting happiness?

GUARD YOUR HEART

TODAY'S PROMISE

Guard your heart above all else, for it determines the course of your life.

—PROVERBS 4:23

TODAY'S THOUGHT

Be careful to guard your heart against temptation because your heart is the center of your desires and affections. Your heart is especially vulnerable because it is easily swayed by emotion, and emotions aren't always rational. If you are caught up in the emotions of the moment, your heart might urge you to feed those feelings, even if it leads you to do something wrong. God promises that guarding your heart will lead you in the way you should go.

TODAY'S PLAN

In what area is your heart most vulnerable? How can you protect it from giving in to the wrong things?

PROMISES OF GOD

TODAY'S PROMISE

Because of his glory and excellence, he has given us great and precious promises. These are the promises that enable you to share his divine nature and escape the world's corruption caused by human desires. In view of all this, make every effort to respond to God's promises. —2 PETER 1:4-5

TODAY'S THOUGHT

Too often our own limitations cause us to doubt God's ability to work through us. It's easy to think up reasons for why things can't happen instead of thinking about how they might happen because our almighty God is involved. The next time you think a promise from God is too impossible to come true, or you are facing a seemingly impossible problem, look at it from God's perspective and ask him to do the impossible! He promises that at the right moment, he can and will do the impossible in you.

TODAY'S PLAN

Which of God's promises seem too impossible to believe?

EFFORT

TODAY'S PROMISE

He trains my hands for battle; he strengthens my arm to draw a bronze bow. . . . I chased my enemies and destroyed them; I did not stop until they were conquered. . . . I struck them down so they did not get up; they fell beneath my feet. . . . You have armed me with strength for the battle; you have subdued my enemies under my feet.

—2 SAMUEL 22:35, 38-40

TODAY'S THOUGHT

Ultimately it is God who grants success. But God expects you to use the strength and abilities he has given you. These verses beautifully describe the interplay between human exertion ("I chased," "I struck them down") and divine provision ("You have armed me with strength," "you have subdued my enemies"). You can trust that when you give your best effort, God will give you victory.

TODAY'S PLAN

How can you give your best effort to use well what God has given you?

VICTORY

TODAY'S PROMISE

The Lord is faithful; he will strengthen you and guard you from the evil one. —2 THESSALONIANS 3:3

The Lord will deliver me from every evil attack and will bring me safely into his heavenly Kingdom.

—2 TIMOTHY 4:18

TODAY'S THOUGHT

You must resist and fight Satan and his demons, for you are in the middle of a spiritual battle. As soon as you became a Christian, they began to attack you, trying to conquer your heart and turn you against God. The battle is over your very soul, so you must fight with all your strength and every weapon God gives you. You cannot defeat Satan while you live on this earth, but Jesus has already won the victory. When you trust him to fight for you, you will be victorious in this life and in eternity.

TODAY'S PLAN

Are you losing the battle, or are you expecting God to give you victory, both now and forever?

DECISIONS

TODAY'S PROMISE

If you need wisdom, ask our generous God, and he will give it to you. He will not rebuke you for asking. But when you ask him, be sure that your faith is in God alone.

—JAMES 1:5-6

TODAY'S THOUGHT

Some people fear they are bothering God when they come to him with their problems. Nothing could be further from the truth. God wants to help you because he loves you. When you ask him for wisdom, he releases his resources to you. If you try to do things without God, you are only able to make decisions out of your limited human knowledge. With God, your decisions can be based on the unlimited knowledge and power of the Almighty.

TODAY'S PLAN

Do you ask God for wisdom in making decisions?

WAR

TODAY'S PROMISE

The LORD will mediate between peoples and will settle disputes between strong nations far away. They will hammer their swords into plowshares and their spears into pruning hooks. Nation will no longer fight against nation, nor train for war anymore. —MICAH 4:3

TODAY'S THOUGHT

There will come a day—the day Jesus returns—when war will be abolished forever. Imagine living in a world with no more fighting, violence, or bloodshed. This promise brings great comfort and joy, for you know that your eternal future will be one of lasting peace.

TODAY'S PLAN

Can you imagine a world without war?

TRUST

TODAY'S PROMISE

Whatever is good and perfect comes down to us from God our Father. . . . He never changes or casts a shifting shadow. He chose to give birth to us by giving us his true word. And we, out of all creation, became his prized possession.

—JAMES 1:17–18

TODAY'S THOUGHT

We trust only those who are dependable, who can be counted on to tell the truth. God didn't just create truth; he *is* truth. Therefore, God cannot lie. Because God cannot lie, everything he says in the Bible is true. All of it must be true, or we could not fully trust God. So when you read God's promises in the Bible, you will discover how much he loves you and wants a close relationship with you. When you trust him with your whole heart, he will make himself known to you in amazing and powerful ways.

TODAY'S PLAN

What steps can you take to trust God more each day?

SPIRITUAL DRYNESS

TODAY'S PROMISE

The LORD will guide you continually, giving you water when you are dry and restoring your strength. You will be like a well-watered garden, like an ever-flowing spring.

—ISAIAH 58:11

TODAY'S THOUGHT

We've all experienced that parched feeling, when we long for a cup of cold water. Our souls can become dry, too, thirsting for something that will truly fulfill us. Seasons of drought come upon our spiritual life when we experience the blazing pressures of the world or the heat of temptation. Just as God sends rain to refresh the earth, he also sends us opportunities to revive our passion and purpose for him. When you see the chance to refresh your soul, you must take it. Don't let the dryness cause unnecessary damage to your faith.

TODAY'S PLAN

Are you thirsting for God?

BROKENNESS

TODAY'S PROMISE

The LORD is close to the brokenhearted; he rescues those whose spirits are crushed.

—PSALM 34:18

TODAY'S THOUGHT

When we are at the end of our rope, we long for God to rescue us. But we would never experience the thrill of being rescued, the utter grace of God's love, if we didn't first experience trouble and hopelessness. Brokenness allows you to experience the overwhelming love of God as he reaches down to rescue you. You are broken when you acknowledge you can't fix things on your own. Then when God comes to the rescue, it will be obvious that his power, not your own, saved you.

TODAY'S PLAN

Do you need to be broken before you can experience a breakthrough with God?

ADDICTION

TODAY'S PROMISE

[Jesus] sat down, called the twelve disciples over to him, and said, "Whoever wants to be first must take last place and be the servant of everyone else." —MARK 9:35

TODAY'S THOUGHT

Addiction gradually causes you to spend more and more time trying to meet your own "needs" and less and less time meeting the needs of others. According to Jesus, however, the Christian life involves serving others, meeting their needs before your own. Addiction focuses you on yourself and causes you to neglect those you love. But the more you put others ahead of yourself, the more God will lift you up.

TODAY'S PLAN

In what areas do you put your needs ahead of the needs of others? How might that lead to an addiction?

MISTAKES

TODAY'S PROMISE

He has removed our sins as far from us as the east is from the west.

—PSALM 103:12

TODAY'S THOUGHT

There can be a difference between making a mistake and committing a sin. For example, accidentally miscalculating your taxes is a mistake. Fudging the numbers to get a bigger tax refund is a sin. You can often avoid repeating a mistake by studying where you went wrong in the past, planning better, and double-checking your words and actions. But to avoid repeating a sin, you need God's help. The regret you feel over a sin indicates that you want to change your ways. When you confess your sin to God, he promises to change you by removing your sin and your regret.

TODAY'S PLAN

Have you asked God to help you avoid both careless mistakes and outright sins?

THOUGHTS

TODAY'S PROMISE

Fix your thoughts on what is true, and honorable, and right, and pure, and lovely, and admirable. Think about things that are excellent and worthy of praise.

—PHILIPPIANS 4:8

TODAY'S THOUGHT

A habit of ungodly thinking will lead to a habit of sinful living. You can change the way you think by focusing your thoughts on God, who is true, honorable, right, pure, lovely, admirable, excellent, and worthy of your praise. Then your godly thinking will turn into a habit of godly living. God promises to help you change your thoughts to good thoughts, which will lead to good actions that bless others.

TODAY'S PLAN

What are your thoughts most often focused on?

FORGETTING

TODAY'S PROMISE

The same happens to all who forget God. The hopes of the godless evaporate. Their confidence hangs by a thread. They are leaning on a spider's web. —JOB 8:13-14

TODAY'S THOUGHT

When you forget God, you have nothing left but sin and yourself, which leaves you no hope for your eternal future. Forgetting God will turn you over to the consequences of sin without the benefits of God's gracious mercy. So you don't forget God, remember how you have seen his hand at work in your past, tell others what he is doing in your life now, and meditate on his Word to see how he promises to work in your future.

TODAY'S PLAN

Are you in danger of forgetting about God?

FAITHFULNESS

TODAY'S PROMISE

On the judgment day, fire will reveal what kind of work each builder has done. The fire will show if a person's work has any value. If the work survives, that builder will receive a reward. But if the work is burned up, the builder will suffer great loss. The builder will be saved, but like someone barely escaping through a wall of flames. —1 CORINTHIANS 3:13-15

TODAY'S THOUGHT

While all who believe in Jesus Christ will inherit eternal life, God promises to give additional rewards and blessings that are based on your obedience and your good deeds in this life. Those who are faithful with what they are given will receive greater blessings.

TODAY'S PLAN

How can you work toward greater faithfulness in things that have eternal value?

UNDERSTANDING

TODAY'S PROMISE

May you experience the love of Christ, though it is too great to understand fully. Then you will be made complete with all the fullness of life and power that comes from God.

—EPHESIANS 3:19

TODAY'S THOUGHT

The Bible promises that God's love is so great, we can never fully understand it. When your heart is filled with the love of Jesus, there won't be room for sin to enter. His love keeps growing inside you, pushing out anything that shouldn't be there. One day, when you reach heaven, God's love will completely fill your heart, and you will have complete understanding of his love and power.

TODAY'S PLAN

Are you looking forward to a complete understanding of God's love?

ADVERSITY

TODAY'S PROMISE

He will be called: Wonderful Counselor, Mighty God, Everlasting Father, Prince of Peace. His government and its peace will never end. He will rule with fairness and justice from the throne of his ancestor David for all eternity. The passionate commitment of the LORD of Heaven's Armies will make this happen!

—ISAIAH 9:6-7

TODAY'S THOUGHT

Adversity is called by a multitude of names—accidents, afflictions, difficulties, disappointments, disasters, failures, hard times, hurts, miseries, misfortunes, sufferings, tragedies, trials, tribulations, woes. But God also has many names—Wonderful Counselor, Mighty God, Everlasting Father, Prince of Peace, Lord of Heaven's Armies, and many more. His names express his greatness. When adversity comes, trust in the magnitude of God's character and his commitment to help you.

TODAY'S PLAN

Which of God's names do you find most comforting during times of adversity?

OPPORTUNITIES

TODAY'S PROMISE

Pharaoh said to Joseph, "Since God has revealed the meaning of the dreams to you, clearly no one else is as intelligent or wise as you are. You will be in charge of my court, and all my people will take orders from you."

—GENESIS 41:39-40

TODAY'S THOUGHT

How you handle each of your responsibilities, big or small, determines whether or not you will be trusted with more. Joseph could have become bitter and done nothing. Instead, he quickly earned others' trust and eventually rose to great prominence in Egypt. When you handle even your minor, day-to-day responsibilities well, you can expect much greater opportunities.

TODAY'S PLAN

How responsible are you in handling every opportunity, both big and small?

FAILURE

TODAY'S PROMISE

Though I fall, I will rise again. Though I sit in darkness, the LORD will be my light. —MICAH 7:8

We are hunted down, but never abandoned by God. We get knocked down, but we are not destroyed.

—2 CORINTHIANS 4:9

TODAY'S THOUGHT

When you fail, you must get up again. God promises to help you if you let him. Many inspiring success stories are about people who failed many times but never gave up. It is most important to avoid failure in your relationship with God. When you succeed in trusting in him, he promises you the ultimate victory of eternal life in the perfect world of heaven.

TODAY'S PLAN

Are you having trouble getting back up after a recent failure? Have you asked God to help you?

THANKFULNESS

TODAY'S PROMISE

Be thankful in all circumstances, for this is God's will for you who belong to Christ Jesus. —1 THESSALONIANS 5:18

TODAY'S THOUGHT

Your loving wife works hard all day, either at work or at home. Do you bother to say thanks? Think about how often in a day other people do things for you, however small. Do you remember to thank them? Now think about how often God helps you in your daily life. Think about how much God has given you. When you pause to think about it, you will see that God is continually blessing you, providing for you, and protecting you. How often do you say thanks to him? Giving thanks is a way to celebrate both the giver and the gift. Remember to thank God in everything.

TODAY'S PLAN

How often do you thank God for the blessings in your life?

THANKFULNESS

TODAY'S PROMISE

Giving thanks is a sacrifice that truly honors me. If you keep to my path, I will reveal to you the salvation of God.
—PSALM 50:23

TODAY'S THOUGHT

Giving thanks to God shows an attitude of gratitude. Having a thankful heart means honoring God for what he has done and recognizing his work, mercy, provision, and blessing in your life. A thankful heart gives you a positive attitude because it keeps you focused on everything God is doing for you instead of on what you think you lack. Make giving thanks to God a part of your daily prayer time. It will be a sacrifice of love that honors God and brings his blessing.

TODAY'S PLAN

Is thanking God a regular part of your daily life?

WORDS

TODAY'S PROMISE

If you claim to be religious but don't control your tongue, you are fooling yourself, and your religion is worthless.

—JAMES 1:26

TODAY'S THOUGHT

Exercising self-control over your words includes discernment in both what you shouldn't say and what you should say. How often do you even take notice of what comes out of your mouth? Ask a friend to help you make a list of the positive and negative words you typically speak. To stop the negative words, before you say something ask yourself, "Is it true? Is it kind? Is it helpful?" If you can answer yes to these questions, your positive words will have an amazing impact on others.

TODAY'S PLAN

How can you make sure you have more positive than negative words coming from your mouth and heart?

CONSEQUENCES

TODAY'S PROMISE

Don't be misled—you cannot mock the justice of God. You will always harvest what you plant. Those who live only to satisfy their own sinful nature will harvest decay and death from that sinful nature. But those who live to please the Spirit will harvest everlasting life from the Spirit. —GALATIANS 6:7-8

TODAY'S THOUGHT

A consequence is an outcome, an aftermath, or a result. Some actions produce consequences that are neither morally good nor bad. For example, if you take a shower, you will get clean. But many thoughts and actions have definite good or bad consequences. Sin will always cause bad consequences. Faithfulness to God will always result in good consequences. Before you act, ask yourself, *What will the consequences of my actions be?*

TODAY'S PLAN

Have you thought through the consequences of what you plan to do and say today?

WISDOM

TODAY'S PROMISE

Fear of the LORD is the foundation of true wisdom.
All who obey his commandments will grow in wisdom.

—PSALM 111:10

TODAY'S THOUGHT

Wisdom is not simply knowing facts and figures; it is understanding how those facts and figures should be used. A person with wisdom recognizes that an all-powerful, all-knowing God has designed a moral universe with consequences for both good and bad choices. Wisdom begins with understanding your accountability to God and your full dependence on your Creator. It's not about what you know but who you know.

The more you know God, the wiser you will become.

TODAY'S PLAN

How well do you know the God of wisdom?

SEDUCTION

TODAY'S PROMISE

Do not let sin control the way you live; do not give in to sinful desires. Do not let any part of your body become an instrument of evil to serve sin. Instead, give yourselves completely to God, for you were dead, but now you have new life. So use your whole body as an instrument to do what is right for the glory of God.

—ROMANS 6:12-13

TODAY'S THOUGHT

Most often we think of seduction within the context of a sexual encounter, but it is actually a tactic that Satan often uses to disguise sin with beauty, power, riches, pleasure, even good deeds. Seduction tempts us to accept an immediate high in exchange for hurtful and even devastating long-term consequences. Seduction takes something that is good out of context and turns it into sin. When you give your whole self—both body and soul—to God, you will have the power to do what is right instead of giving in to seduction.

TODAY'S PLAN

Is Satan trying to seduce you right now?

CREATION

TODAY'S PROMISE

It is the LORD who provides the sun to light the day and the moon and stars to light the night, and who stirs the sea into roaring waves. His name is the LORD of Heaven's Armies.
— JEREMIAH 31:35

TODAY'S THOUGHT

Who but the Creator can control creation? All of creation is a testimony to the powerful hand of God. The facts of creation—that the sun comes up and warms you, that the rain waters the land, that the seasons continue without fail—reveal a God who still holds the world in his loving and powerful hands.

TODAY'S PLAN

How can you let the wonders of creation remind you of the Creator's care today?

DECEMBER

EXAMPLE

TODAY'S PROMISE

Take a new grip with your tired hands and strengthen your weak knees. Mark out a straight path for your feet so that those who are weak and lame will not fall but become strong.

—HEBREWS 12:12-13

TODAY'S THOUGHT

You don't have to be perfect to be an example of godliness to others. Often it is those who overcome the most adversity and remain faithful to God that are the best examples of God's love, strength, and power. When you resolve to live for God, to stand firm on your convictions, and to obey his commands, people around you will be inspired by your example of faith as they clearly see God's work in your life.

TODAY'S PLAN

Is your life a good example to others of God's strength and love at work?

SPIRITUAL WARFARE

TODAY'S PROMISE

Be strong in the Lord and in his mighty power. Put on all of God's armor so that you will be able to stand firm against all strategies of the devil. For we are not fighting against flesh-and-blood enemies, but against evil rulers and authorities of the unseen world, against mighty powers in this dark world, and against evil spirits in the heavenly places.

—EPHESIANS 6:10-12

TODAY'S THOUGHT

Since the fall of humankind, the earth has not known a time without the influence of evil. We face an enemy far more powerful than any human foe—Satan, the very embodiment of evil. His goal is for evil to triumph. But God has given us powerful weapons and armor to fight against the forces of evil. And he has promised victory to all those who believe in him.

TODAY'S PLAN

Have you asked God to outfit you in the fight against evil?

TIMING OF GOD

TODAY'S PROMISE

When we were utterly helpless, Christ came at just the right time and died for us sinners. —ROMANS 5:6

TODAY'S THOUGHT

God's people had been longing for the Messiah for centuries, yet God sent Jesus to earth at just the right time. We may not fully understand why this was perfect timing until we get to heaven and see God's complete plan. But you can be sure that God sent Jesus at the time when the most people, both present and future, would be reached with the Good News of salvation.

TODAY'S PLAN

How does God's perfect timing in sending Jesus assure you of his perfect timing in your life?

CHALLENGES

TODAY'S PROMISE

In your strength I can crush an army; with my God I can scale any wall. —2 SAMUEL 22:30

TODAY'S THOUGHT

Challenges keep you from getting too comfortable or too accepting of the status quo; they force you into uncharted waters. Without God's leading, this would be frightening, but with God it can be a great adventure. So whatever challenge you are facing, make sure you head into it with God at your side.

TODAY'S PLAN

What challenge is keeping you from getting comfortable? Try to picture God by your side, and then move forward with confidence.

GIFTS

TODAY'S PROMISE

God loved the world so much that he gave his one and only Son, so that everyone who believes in him will not perish but have eternal life.

—JOHN 3:16

TODAY'S THOUGHT

The greatest gift God gives you is his Son. Through his gift of Jesus, he also gives you the gift of eternal life. What makes these gifts so wonderful is that you don't have to work for them or earn them. You simply believe that God has actually given you his Son and the offer of eternal life with him. Then you accept the gifts. And no one can take them away.

TODAY'S PLAN

God has given you gifts too wonderful to keep to yourself. Whom can you share them with?

SATISFACTION

TODAY'S PROMISE

Is anyone thirsty? Come and drink—even if you have no money! Come, take your choice of wine or milk—it's all free! Why spend your money on food that does not give you strength? Why pay for food that does you no good? Listen to me, and you will eat what is good. You will enjoy the finest food. —ISAIAH 55:1-2

TODAY'S THOUGHT

Satisfaction is a soul issue. Anytime you seek satisfaction from a source other than God, you will be dissatisfied. The hunger for God that all people have cannot be satisfied with accomplishments, hard work, wealth, fame, or other worldly goods. These may bring temporary satisfaction, but they are not lasting sources of soul satisfaction. You can't feed your soul with worldly food. It can only be satisfied with spiritual food from God.

TODAY'S PLAN

Are you feeding your soul with the right things?

COMPASSION

TODAY'S PROMISE

Feed the hungry, and help those in trouble. Then your light will shine out from the darkness, and the darkness around you will be as bright as noon. —ISAIAH 58:10

TODAY'S THOUGHT

God promises that those who help the poor will be rewarded, both in this life and in the next. God has compassion for the poor and needy, so as a follower of God, you must also have compassion for them. Compassion that does not reach as far as your checkbook or your to-do list is not godly compassion. Godly compassion requires action. Helping those less fortunate than you is not merely an obligation but a privilege that should bring you great joy.

TODAY'S PLAN

What can you can do this week to show compassion to someone who is poor or needy?

EXCUSES

TODAY'S PROMISE

"But Lord," Gideon replied, "how can I rescue Israel? My clan is the weakest in the whole tribe of Manasseh, and I am the least in my entire family!" The LORD said to him, "I will be with you."

—JUDGES 6:15-16

TODAY'S THOUGHT

Gideon thought he had a good excuse to get out of serving God. But the qualifications God looks for are different from what we might expect. He often chooses the least likely people to do his work in order to demonstrate his power more effectively. If you know God has called you to do something, stop trying to excuse yourself. He promises to give you the help and strength you need to get the job done.

TODAY'S PLAN

Are you making excuses to get out of something God wants you to do?

ATTITUDE

TODAY'S PROMISE

Since you have heard about Jesus and have learned the truth that comes from him, throw off your old sinful nature and your former way of life, which is corrupted by lust and deception. Instead, let the Spirit renew your thoughts and attitudes. Put on your new nature, created to be like God—truly righteous and holy.

—EPHESIANS 4:21-24

TODAY'S THOUGHT

God is changing you from the inside out, starting with your thoughts and attitudes. The most important part of having a good attitude is refusing to yield to your sinful nature, which would cause you to go back to your old way of living. With God's help, you can actually think yourself into a new way of living and live yourself into a new way of thinking!

TODAY'S PLAN

How is God changing your attitude?

RECONCILIATION

TODAY'S PROMISE

God was in Christ, reconciling the world to himself, no longer counting people's sins against them. And he gave us this wonderful message of reconciliation. . . . For God made Christ, who never sinned, to be the offering for our sin, so that we could be made right with God through Christ. —2 CORINTHIANS 5:19-21

TODAY'S THOUGHT

All people are born with a sinful nature, and sin separates us from God. If you want a personal relationship with him, you must be reconciled to him. That begins with the recognition that without the work of Jesus Christ on the cross, you cannot approach God. God chose to have his Son, Jesus, take your punishment so you could come to him. When you accept God's gift of salvation, you are reconciled to him and can begin a relationship with him. Salvation is the greatest gift you could ever receive, and it is the only way to be reconciled to God.

TODAY'S PLAN

Have you been reconciled to God?

RESTLESSNESS

TODAY'S PROMISE

Therefore, since we have been made right in God's sight by faith, we have peace with God because of what Jesus Christ our Lord has done for us. —ROMANS 5:1

TODAY'S THOUGHT

Feelings of restlessness range from indecision to impatience to lack of purpose. It is like being lost; you know there is some place you are supposed to be, but you can't or don't know how to get there. Restlessness can only be cured by finding peace with God. You find peace with God by allowing him to direct you to where you need to be. Don't worry about where you are going or how you will get there—he will take you there. Then you will be confident in your decisions, patient in hard times, and purposeful in everything you do.

TODAY'S PLAN

Do you feel restless? Are you at peace with God?

EXAMPLE

TODAY'S PROMISE

Now I am giving you a new commandment: Love each other. Just as I have loved you, you should love each other. Your love for one another will prove to the world that you are my disciples. —JOHN 13:34-35

TODAY'S THOUGHT

Regardless of the level of your gifts and abilities, God wants you to invest what he's given you into the lives of others. He promises that when you follow his example of love and service, you will become an example to others of Christ's love. Your example will even change the lives of many other people.

TODAY'S PLAN

What can you do to be an example of Christ's love and service today?

LONELINESS

TODAY'S PROMISE

The more we suffer for Christ, the more God will shower us with his comfort through Christ. —2 CORINTHIANS 1:5

TODAY'S THOUGHT

There may be times when you feel alone in your faith. Others may mock you or oppose you because of your faith in God. But God promises to lavish his comfort on those who suffer for him. Times of loneliness can be special opportunities from God that will lead you to experience the joy of drawing closer to him. Trust in God's promise of comfort to get you through your loneliness.

TODAY'S PLAN

Do you feel alone in your faith? How can you use this time to draw closer to God?

CHARACTER

TODAY'S PROMISE

The more you grow like this, the more productive and useful you will be in your knowledge of our Lord Jesus Christ. —2 PETER 1:8

TODAY'S THOUGHT

Character is what you are, but it is also what you want to become. Ultimately, your character is the mark you make on the world around you. If you are striving for good character—better yet, for godly character—you are working toward moral excellence. Think of all the areas in your life, such as career or hobbies, in which you've worked hard to develop excellence. Doesn't it also make sense to work hard at becoming morally excellent, mastering the things that really matter, such as integrity, kindness, love, and faithfulness? You can do that by asking God to work through you as you relate to others.

TODAY'S PLAN

Your reputation, or what other people say about you, is often a good measure of your character. If you could hear others talking about you, what might they be saying?

GIFTS

TODAY'S PROMISE

A spiritual gift is given to each of us so we can help each other. . . . It is the one and only Spirit who distributes all these gifts. He alone decides which gift each person should have. —1 CORINTHIANS 12:7, 11

TODAY'S THOUGHT

Why do we give gifts? Because gifts are a symbol of our love, commitment, and care for others. When we find the perfect gift for a friend or loved one, it gives us great joy to see that person delight in it. Similarly, God handpicks special gifts for each one of us, and he takes great delight when we use those gifts for his glory. Some of his gifts to us are spiritual gifts. You never use up these spiritual gifts; the more you use them, the more they grow and help you make a greater contribution in your sphere of influence. They are a symbol of God's deep, personal, and attentive love and commitment to you.

TODAY'S PLAN

What spiritual gift has God given you? How will you use it today?

SHARING

TODAY'S PROMISE

When Christ, who is your life, is revealed to the whole world, you will share in all his glory. —COLOSSIANS 3:4

TODAY'S THOUGHT

Ever since we were little children, we've been taught to share. Yet for most of us, it remains as hard as ever to share either our things or ourselves. Why? Because at the very core of our sinful human nature is the desire to get, not give; to accumulate, not relinquish; to look out for ourselves, not for others. The Bible calls you to share many things—your resources, your faith, your love, your time, your talents, your money. It promises that those who share generously will discover the benefits of giving, which are far greater than the temporary satisfaction of receiving. God was willing to share his own Son with you so that you could have eternal life. When you realize how much God has shared with you, you will be more willing to share with others to bless their lives.

TODAY'S PLAN

What do you have that you can share generously with others?

PEACE

TODAY'S PROMISE

A child is born to us, a son is given to us. The government will rest on his shoulders. And he will be called: Wonderful Counselor, Mighty God, Everlasting Father, Prince of Peace.

—ISAIAH 9:6

TODAY'S THOUGHT

Lasting peace comes only from Jesus Christ, the Prince of Peace. Because he rules over all creation, as well as over your life, you can be sure that one day he will bring complete peace on earth. Until then, he offers you peace of mind and heart when you give him control of your life. You can have peace knowing that your life is in the hands of a loving God who is passionately committed to you.

TODAY'S PLAN

Do you search for peace within yourself or from the Prince of Peace?

CONNECTED

TODAY'S PROMISE

[Jesus said,] "Remain in me, and I will remain in you. For a branch cannot produce fruit if it is severed from the vine, and you cannot be fruitful unless you remain in me. Yes, I am the vine; you are the branches. Those who remain in me, and I in them, will produce much fruit." —JOHN 15:4-5

TODAY'S THOUGHT

When you are connected to Jesus, he turns your acts of service into something profound and purposeful. For example, he turns your simple act of singing into a profound chorus of praise that ministers to an entire congregation. He turns your testimony of faith into a profound moment in the heart of a friend who suddenly realizes his need for salvation. Stay connected to Jesus, and let him turn your acts of service into profound works for the Kingdom of God.

TODAY'S PLAN

What simple act of service can you do for Jesus today?

RISK

TODAY'S PROMISE

Mary responded, "I am the Lord's servant. May everything you have said about me come true." And then the angel left her. —LUKE 1:38

TODAY'S THOUGHT

Take the risk of doing things God's way. When God asks you to follow him, he won't necessarily give you all the information up front. When you step out in faith, he gives you just enough guidance to see where to take the next step. Mary risked her marriage, her reputation, and her future by becoming the mother of Jesus. Following God's will is not without risks, but God promises that it brings the greatest reward.

TODAY'S PLAN

How much risk are you willing to take in following God?

PURITY

TODAY'S PROMISE

Who may climb the mountain of the LORD? Who may stand in his holy place? Only those whose hands and hearts are pure. —PSALM 24:3-4

TODAY'S THOUGHT

Purity means being like Jesus in thoughts, words, and actions. While you can never be fully free from sin in this life, you can still strive for purity. God promises to honor and bless those who strive to have a pure heart because it demonstrates a sincere commitment to be like Jesus.

TODAY'S PLAN

Are you striving for purity each day?

GOOD NEWS

TODAY'S PROMISE

How beautiful on the mountains are the feet of the messenger who brings good news, the good news of peace and salvation, the news that the God of Israel reigns!

—ISAIAH 52:7

TODAY'S THOUGHT

The Good News of Jesus the Messiah is that you will find joy and peace when you develop a relationship with him. He came to earth as a human so he could relate to humans. Now he is preparing a place where we will one day live forever with him in peace. The Bible promises an added measure of joy when you share the Good News with others.

TODAY'S PLAN

How can your life be a living testimony of the Good News, the joy and peace you have through a relationship with Jesus?

POWER OF GOD

TODAY'S PROMISE

The Mighty One is holy, and he has done great things for me. He shows mercy from generation to generation to all who fear him. His mighty arm has done tremendous things!

—LUKE 1:49-51

The Son radiates God's own glory and expresses the very character of God, and he sustains everything by the mighty power of his command.

—HEBREWS 1:3

TODAY'S THOUGHT

It's hard to picture the baby Jesus as the almighty God, but he was mighty enough to create the world, live a sinless life, heal countless people, calm storms, and conquer death. He is mighty enough to conquer your troubles, too, no matter how overwhelming your circumstances.

TODAY'S PLAN

Do you more readily see Jesus as the baby in the manger or as the almighty God?

HUMILITY

TODAY'S PROMISE

The Savior—yes, the Messiah, the Lord—has been born today in Bethlehem, the city of David! And . . . you will find a baby wrapped snugly in strips of cloth, lying in a manger.

—LUKE 2:11-12

TODAY'S THOUGHT

God often accomplishes his plans in unexpected ways. He used the census to bring Joseph and Mary to Bethlehem. He chose to have Jesus born in a stable rather than in a palace; he chose Bethlehem rather than Jerusalem; and he chose to proclaim the news of Jesus' birth first to shepherds rather than to kings. Perhaps God did all this to show that life's greatest treasure—salvation through Jesus—is available to everyone, no matter what their status.

TODAY'S PLAN

Have you accepted the salvation that Jesus brings to all people?

GIFTS

TODAY'S PROMISE

A good person produces good things from the treasury of a good heart, and an evil person produces evil things from the treasury of an evil heart. —MATTHEW 12:35

TODAY'S THOUGHT

It is often said of gifts, "It's the thought that counts." When it comes to giving gifts to God, it might be said, "It's the heart that counts." Often the greatest gifts you can offer him are not monetary or material but personal and sacrificial gifts of service, time, and talent.

TODAY'S PLAN

Can you offer your heart as a gift to God today?

SALVATION

TODAY'S PROMISE

God saved you by his grace when you believed. And you can't take credit for this; it is a gift from God.

—EPHESIANS 2:8

TODAY'S THOUGHT

It seems too good to be true: The greatest gift God could ever offer—salvation and eternal life in a perfect world—is absolutely free! You can accept this free gift by (1) admitting your sin, (2) acknowledging that your sin cuts you off from God, (3) asking Jesus to forgive your sins, and (4) believing that Jesus is your Savior and Lord and that he is the Son of God. God's gift of salvation is yours—and it's one offer you can actually believe in!

TODAY'S PLAN

Have your accepted God's greatest gift?

CELEBRATION

TODAY'S PROMISE

This festival will be a happy time of celebrating with your sons and daughters . . . to honor the LORD your God . . . for it is he who blesses you with bountiful harvests and gives you success in all your work.

—DEUTERONOMY 16:14-15

TODAY'S THOUGHT

The Bible teaches that celebration is both important and necessary. Celebration gives you the opportunity to experience the joy of work, the satisfaction and rewards of accomplishment, and the good things of creation. It encourages a spirit of gratitude and renews your energy for the work yet to be done. Even when a celebration comes to an end, you can continue to celebrate the joys of your friends, your family, and your relationship with Jesus Christ.

TODAY'S PLAN

Now that Christmas is over, what can you continue to celebrate?

PURPOSE

TODAY'S PROMISE

I cry out to God Most High, to God who will fulfill his purpose for me.

—PSALM 57:2

TODAY'S THOUGHT

Purpose comes from obeying God and doing his will—his will for all believers, which is found in the Bible, and his specific will for you, which you can discover through prayer and a deepening relationship with him. The ultimate purpose of your life is not to reach the destinations you want to go to but the ones God wants for you.

TODAY'S PLAN

Have you asked God where he wants your life to go?

GOALS

TODAY'S PROMISE

Take delight in the LORD, and he will give you your heart's desires.
—PSALM 37:4

TODAY'S THOUGHT

As you think about setting goals for the coming year, here's a place to start: Make a commitment to learning how to apply your faith to everyday life and to become more confident about what you believe. When you pursue these goals, you'll find that the other priorities in your life will fall neatly into place because there will be no conflict between what you believe and what you do.

TODAY'S PLAN

Have you ever set goals for your spiritual life before? Make the extra effort to do so this year.

FLEXIBILITY

TODAY'S PROMISE

The wisdom from above is first of all pure. It is also peace loving, gentle at all times, and willing to yield to others.

—JAMES 3:17

TODAY'S THOUGHT

When you have godly wisdom and obey God's Word, it actually allows you to be more flexible. Disobedience shows a stubborn desire to please only yourself, but obeying God shows a desire to follow his call wherever he might lead you.

TODAY'S PLAN

How can you be more flexible in responding to God?

FINISHING WELL

TODAY'S PROMISE

How do you know what your life will be like tomorrow? Your life is like the morning fog—it's here a little while, then it's gone. —JAMES 4:14

Therefore, whenever we have the opportunity, we should do good. —GALATIANS 6:10

TODAY'S THOUGHT

Another year has slipped by, and you wonder where the time went and how it went so quickly. That's why it is so important to do your best each day, whether in your work, your relation- ships, or your walk with God. Be faithful to carry out the responsibilities and the calling that God will give you in the new year to come. Then at the end of next year, you will have the satisfaction of finishing a job well done and experiencing the pleasure of God.

TODAY'S PLAN

Have you finished well this year? What goals can you set now so that you will finish well next year too?

FINISHING WELL

TODAY'S PROMISE

I am certain that God, who began the good work within you, will continue his work until it is finally finished on the day when Christ Jesus returns.

—PHILIPPIANS 1:6

TODAY'S THOUGHT

Don't fail to finish what God starts in your life. If he convicts you of a sin, root it out of your life; don't allow it to linger in your heart and mind. If he opens a door of opportunity, walk through it and pursue his call as diligently as you can. Whatever God starts in your life, you can trust him to help you finish it if you follow through, persevere, and never give up.

TODAY'S PLAN

What good thing has God begun in you? How will you follow through with him to finish it?

TOPICAL INDEX